DINNER THEATRE

DINNER THEATRE
A Survey and Directory

William M. Lynk

GREENWOOD PRESS
Westport, Connecticut • London

Library of Congress Cataloging-in-Publication Data

Lynk, William M.
    Dinner theatre : a survey and directory / William M. Lynk.
        p.   cm.
    Includes index.
    ISBN 0–313–28442–3 (alk. paper)
    1. Dinner theater—United States.   2. Dinner theater—United
States—Directories.   I. Title.
    PN2270.D56L9   1993
    792′.022—dc20   92–36607

British Library Cataloguing in Publication Data is available.

Library of Congress Catalog Card Number: 92–36607
ISBN: 0–313–28442–3

First published in 1993

Greenwood Press, 88 Post Road West, Westport, CT 06881
An imprint of Greenwood Publishing Group, Inc.

Printed in the United States of America

The paper used in this book complies with the
Permanent Paper Standard issued by the National
Information Standards Organization (Z39.48–1984).

10 9 8 7 6 5 4 3 2 1

Contents

Preface

In the thirty-three years of dinner theatre history, it is surprising that no one previously has written a book devoted solely to this multi-million-dollar business. The need is apparent not only for archival purposes, but for the immediate reference value that such a work offers to those directly connected with the industry, to those on its periphery and those interested in learning about it.

The present guide provides a comprehensive overview of all facets of the dinner theatre industry. As such, it includes valuable information for actors, musicians, playwrights, directors, choreographers, food service purveyors, and dinner theatre owners and employees. Written at the nuts-and-bolts level and with practical insights from professionals in the field, the book will also be helpful for those interested in starting a dinner theatre operation. Furthermore, it is a useful resource for those associated in any way with the entertainment spectrum, such as tour operators, motorcoach organizations, travel bureaus, and colleges and universities. Librarians at educational institutions and public libraries will be able to direct queries of students, researchers, and patrons of dinner theatres to this source.

Dinner Theatre: A Survey and Directory begins by examining what dinner theatre is—as presented through a variety of perspectives from those most closely involved with the business. These individuals explain how dinner theatres vary according to the market, the facility, size, and format. Historically, the industry is reviewed, from its origins in Washington, D.C., in 1959 through today.

Considering that half of the dinner theatre concept relies upon the food service area, this integral component is fully explored. How food quality, presentation, and service format differ within dinner theatres is discussed, as are menu types and variations within regions. The "theatre" part of dinner theatre is treated in terms of its importance within the total operation. Vehicles such as musicals and other types of plays are discussed, as are the special attributes, concerns, and needs of directors and actors and other elements critical to producing a dinner theatre production. Business concerns such as utilizing the appropriate budget, union procedures, market differences, start-up and operating costs, and industry trends vital to those closely connected with dinner theatre demonstrate that operating a dinner theatre involves more than simply running a composite restaurant and theatre.

A major focus is directed toward an in-depth look at some of the best-known and most successful dinner theatres in the country. Pertinent statistical information useful to actors, tour operators, producers, food purveyors, and researchers is included. A complete directory of dinner theatres across the country is provided, as is a listing of various informational sources such as associations, unions, rental/royalty houses, periodicals, and suppliers. Any individual working in the dinner theatre industry or someone wishing information regarding this special entertainment genre will find this handbook and directory easy to use and a reliable reference source.

Because of the overall value that was intrinsic from its origin, dinner theatre has surmounted a tumultuous three-decade history and is still evolving to best serve its audiences in accordance with the times. It is the hope of this author that dinner theatre will continue to flourish and remain a source of income, pride, and pleasure for millions in the years to come.

Note: Shortly before this book went to press it was learned that Connecticut's Broadway Theatre had temporarily suspended operation due to financial difficulties. The situation remains unresolved, and the information on the theatre has not, therefore, been changed.

Acknowledgments

Writing a book of this nature takes more time than one can foresee, especially when one is working with hundreds of industry personnel to acquire necessary information. My sincere appreciation is hereby extended to all those individuals who have helped me in creating this "first" in the dinner theatre business. Those in the forefront include: Scott Griffith, Betty Wilson, Jane Bergere, Tony D'Angelo, Bob Funking, Kary Walker, Bill Pullinsi, Tod Booth, Jim Jude, Chris Howland, Virginia Sherwood, Bill Stutler, Diane Van Lente, Tony DeSantis, Josh Cockey, Jan McArt, Johnny Lazzara, Bob Turoff, Mark Turpin, John Chaffin, Mary Simon, J. Test, Bob Bruyr, Chris Von Gronnigen, Sherry Eaker, Tom Walsh, and my Mom and Dad.

DINNER THEATRE

CHAPTER 1

What Is Dinner Theatre?

THE CONCEPT

The concept of "dinner theatre" is quite simple; however, the proper execution of this concept, even in its most basic form, is a complex process. Dinner theatre is the combination of a quality meal and a live theatrical presentation, presumably in the same room, at a value-oriented ticket price. This "total entertainment package under one roof," offering good value, is the cornerstone of the dinner theatre concept.

WHY IT WORKS

Like any industry, dinner theatre has had its ups and downs. Problems still exist along with successes. First, why the idea continues to work shall be examined.

Patrons have supported dinner theatre for several reasons. Most dinner theatres usually cater to the senior citizen market. The seniors are, as many theatre operators are aware, price conscious. Dinner theatre offers them the option of a meal combined with live stage entertainment. In addition, it seems that the general dinner theatre market is gradually expanding to embrace a younger clientele.

Another factor to be considered is that quality productions have always been an attractive feature. Some dinner theatres utilize local non-union actors who are well trained and experienced, providing good entertainment at a reasonable cost. Other dinner theatres employ union actors, those who are strictly professional stage actors working across the country. Many of these performers have had experience on Broadway, off Broadway, with national tours, in summer stock, and in regional theatre.

One can't forget the other half of dinner theatre: the food. Many operations serve buffet style, although the current trend is toward table service. In a menu that may range from fried chicken, green beans, and mashed potatoes to filet mignon and lobster, quantity and quality are both important factors to most patrons.

But the main attraction for dinner theatre has always been the low ticket price. It's a superb package deal, considering the quality of what is being offered. A Saturday night ticket price of $29.75 per person, for example, may include dinner, a beverage, a show, parking, and tax. Figured separately, dinner in a comparable restaurant, an Equity show, parking, and taxes may cost the same patron over $70.00! Clearly the package of dinner and theatre is an unbeatable bargain.

WHY IT DOESN'T WORK

When a dinner theatre flourishes, it does so for many of the reasons previously mentioned. But when it doesn't work, it's often because the management is ineffective. The producer/owner of a dinner theatre must have many talents. When the owner focuses only on food service and has no theatrical background, the shows can go "down the tubes." Conversely, producers/owners with a strong theatrical background and no restaurant knowledge can "lose their pants." Dinner theatre is a strange mix of two risky businesses that are combined into an even riskier business. It takes a person with a strong business and management background as well as a theatrical flair to oversee effectively all aspects of a dinner theatre operation.

A dinner theatre may fail if it does not align itself properly with the market it serves. This means scheduling the right mix of shows, considering the trends of the times. Dinner theatres close each year across the country, but many expand and new ones open, signifying that the market is there if the concept is treated properly.

INTO THE 1990s

Dinner theatre has had a roller-coaster ride during its three-decade history. During the 1980s it seemed that there were more dinner theatres closing than new ones being opened. There also has been an image problem that has taken its toll on the industry. When dinner theatre was in its infancy, it began in many places as an offshoot of community theatre using only local talent, serving patrons "greasy spoon"-type buffet food.

It was truly a "bargain package," to say the least. Even though this would not be a fair assessment of the industry today, for many the image lingers.

Most of the union dinner theatres that were thriving in the 1960s and 1970s have either closed since then or gone non-union. In 1978 there were over 70 union dinner theatres; in 1992 there were only about 20. The main reason is economics.

Audiences today have a wide variety of entertainment choices; the competition is fierce. Further, people may be changing along with technology. Is the dinner theatre industry keeping up with these changes? Dinner theatre is in direct competition with cable television, home video rentals, and other entertainment options. But even considering the extraordinary visual special effects created by electronic technology, this can never replace the live theatrical experience.

On the positive side, actors are finding that dinner theatre can provide a great source of acting experience, especially in the competitive markets of New York, Chicago, and Los Angeles. They can portray roles in dinner theatres that they might not get in larger markets. Actors have also noted that salary ranges in the union dinner theatres are competitive with those in other areas of union work available to them. Patrons, moreover, are returning to dinner theatres to dine and see their favorite shows.

In these difficult economic times, when there is a plethora of entertainment options, it is the bargain-priced events that will survive. If costs can be contained, and management proves effective, dinner theatre will continue to flourish and be an important source of income and career experience for the actor, and a memorable dining and theatrical experience for the patron.

COMMON THREADS

There are certain threads that bind successful dinner theatres together. What is seen by the patron is the final work of art: a product that should have aesthetic appeal and be satisfying. The common threads that create this product include excellent productions, hospitality, quality food, exceptional management, and appropriate ambiance.

Various owners have offered descriptions of what they feel are important considerations for operating a top-notch dinner theatre in their own particular markets.

Effective Management

One of the key features of a profitable dinner theatre operation is superior management. John and Dianne Chaffin, owners of Chaffin's Barn in Nashville, Tennessee, agree with the fact that most dinner theatre ills can be traced to poor management and not to the concept itself.

Chaffin's Barn was only the ninth dinner theatre to be launched in the United States when it opened on March 29, 1967. During the first 12 years, the theatre's ownership was kept within the family. In 1979, Chaffin's Barn was purchased by the Highland Inns Corporation. According to the Chaffins, the long-standing reputation developed by their family was quickly soiled by poor management practices and a lack of understanding of the entire dinner theatre concept.

The Highland Inns Corporation changed its name to Advantage Companies, Inc., but continued to suffer heavy losses because of the same lack of effective management. In October of 1983, Advantage sold Chaffin's Barn to an employee, Ken Tanner. With an overwhelming debt due to corporate incompetence, Tanner was forced into bankruptcy and the property was returned to John Chaffin. With this striking example, it's easy to see what doesn't work at a dinner theatre—poor management.

During the first 12 years of its operation, Chaffin's Barn had been considered a complete success in the Nashville market. People travelled from a three-state area each month to enjoy a buffet dinner with a live theatrical presentation. The dinner theatre had grown as a friendly, profitable family business.

Today, Chaffin's Barn has returned to the type of operation begun years ago. Owned again by John and Dianne Chaffin, this non-Equity theatre seats 300 and is in-the-round.

GOING SOUTH

Travelling further south, one comes to the Mark Two Dinner Theatre in Orlando, Florida. Owner/producer Mark Howard says that he has been preparing for his whole life to operate this unique business, which, incidentally, is considered by most financial institutions to be one of the highest-risk businesses in existence. This "risky" business has become a profitable operation in the heart of Florida since Howard purchased the theatre (formerly the Gaslight Theatre and then the Once Upon a Stage Dinner Theatre) in 1986.

Mark Howard is certainly no stranger to the music/theatre industry. For five years, Howard was with the Metropolitan Opera Studio, where he sang with such greats as Luciano Pavarotti, Franco Corelli, and Beverly Sills. To add to his diverse directing and producing credits, Howard also taught music and drama at a number of colleges and music institutes in the United States and in Europe.

With such fierce competition in Orlando, due to the multitude of entertainment options open to the public, how can the Mark Two survive, let alone flourish? "Very simply," Howard answers. "Present an excellent product." Howard explains that from the time the patrons enter, until the time they leave, their entire experience must be a superb one. He feels that food quality, performance standards, and ambiance are all critical in running a successful operation.

The Mark Two is a year-round Equity theatre, seating 320 patrons. Dinner is a buffet and shows are done on a three-quarter thrust stage. Mark Howard also originated a company called Costumes Unlimited, which makes and rents costumes for individuals and for other theatres across the country.

MOVING WEST

Located in an area where the snow falls in December, just off Interstate 25 in southeast Denver, is the Country Dinner Playhouse, where professional, Broadway productions are not just occasional, but the norm. Co-owner Sam Newton founded the 470-seat Playhouse in 1970 along with the late Bob Boren. It was then the first specially built theatre-in-the-round in Denver, and continues to be the only year-round Equity theatre in Colorado.

Sam Newton is happy to have Bill McHale, executive producer/director, as part of the Playhouse. Under the skillful direction of McHale, the Country Dinner Playhouse has won national acclaim for such productions as *Fiddler on the Roof*, *The King and I*, *Evita*, *42nd Street*, and *The Music Man* (whose composer, Meredith Willson, said the Country Dinner Playhouse production of his work was the finest he had ever seen).

McHale feels strongly that one of the main reasons the Country Dinner Playhouse is so successful is the quality of theatre presented. Professional excellence of productions is indeed McHale's main goal. Having launched and nurtured the careers of such notable performers as Ted Shackelford, Morgan Fairchild, and Lee Horsley, he adds, "You can have great food and good service. You can get that almost anywhere, but it's the production quality that must be excellent if our guests are going to return."

Clearly the dinner theatre industry is a people-oriented business. There's no way around it: Proper management and hospitality must be a top priority. At the same time, one shouldn't minimize the professionalism of a production and the quality of the food. The heartbeat of each dinner theatre is the show and dinner, and this thread is connected to all the other aspects. And yet another intertwining thread is the total experience as the patrons perceive it. Their impressions will last long after the curtain falls. What works, then, at a particular dinner theatre is a successful blend of these connecting threads.

INDUSTRY PERSPECTIVES

Dinner theatre is a continually changing industry. From its simple origins to its national acceptance today, good food and quality live entertainment—together at a reasonable price—have established dinner theatre's very special niche in the entertainment world.

In tough economic times, what future does dinner theatre have in the 1990s and beyond? To held answer this question, perspectives are given here not only by owners, but also by music directors, actors, actresses, director/choreographers, food service directors, public relations directors, celebrities, group sales directors and marketing directors.

TOM PRATHER, Owner, Dutch Apple Dinner Theatre, Lancaster, PA

"Every hour of every day, there is a bigger market for the dinner theatre industry. As more people grow older, the new seniors are becoming much more selective in their choices. They want better food, high-quality entertainment, and a clean, fresh facility. They're expecting a first-class operation." Prather, a past president of the National Dinner Theatre Association (NDTA), has been owner of the Dutch Apple, a non-union dinner theatre, since 1987; but he has been producing dinner theatre for 26 years. He feels the future for dinner theatre is extremely bright: "There is a wonderful future for dinner theatre in the nineties. Our customer base will remain an older crowd and we must cater to their needs. Dinner theatre will need to become much more innovative, challenging." What Prather suggests is the presenting of a wider range of show types and balancing them out with the war-horses. He feels that, as the baby boomers eventually become seniors, they will look for a broader range of presentations, as compared to the seniors of today.

Prather explains that each theatre market will determine for itself if buffet food service will be more successful than table service. In either case, more health-oriented foods need to be offered. He notes: "The look of the facility, both inside and outside, must be fresh and appealing—including clean and ample restrooms. Service should be friendly—attentive and pleasant. Look at Walt Disney World and how successful it is. Customer satisfaction is number one. It's definitely my role model."

BRENDAN J. SHEEHAN, Music Director, West End Dinner Theatre, Alexandria, VA

Brendan Sheehan has been part of musical theatre for twelve years, and has been with the non-union West End Dinner Theatre for four years as music director. He feels there have been significant changes in the area of instrumental music within the dinner theatre circuit. He says: "It seems that pit orchestras with about four-to-six people are now used, or the dinner theatre may use only taped music. The small non-Equity theatres can't afford to pay the musicians on an ongoing basis, so they are using tapes unless a special budget is set aside for a particular show." According to Sheehan, the D.C. crowd will pay the price to see a quality show. They are more selective about where they will go for entertainment; therefore, the competition has greatly increased. The show itself is the real draw, as opposed to the food-and-show package deal that dinner theatre has always offered.

Even though Sheehan foresees a heavier use of tapes and synthesizers on the dinner theatre circuit, he feels there are definite advantages in utilizing live musicians: "The singers work well with live musicians. It encourages musical growth during the run and it makes them feel more secure artistically. It also allows the ensemble the ability to adjust to the audience, as well as to the pace of the performance itself." Using tapes, however, compensates for varying degrees of acting talent; for the newer actors, it helps keep them in line. Tapes also are consistent in pace and tempo. Tapes give a great sound to the overtures of the larger musicals—a sound that can be difficult to achieve with a very small pit orchestra. Obviously, using tapes is much less costly than hiring live musicians. Regarding the future, Sheehan feels that synthesizers will be used either to make tapes or in lieu of tapes. Synthesizers are definitely the trend.

GEORGE CHAKIRIS, International Star of Stage and Screen, Los Angeles

After completing his eight-week role as Harold Hill in *The Music Man* at the 1,130-seat Carousel Dinner Theatre in Akron, Ohio, George Chakiris said he is able to "stay in shape" by doing stage work. Best known for his Oscar-winning role as Bernardo in the film version of *West Side Story*, Chakiris also appeared in such great films as *There's No Business Like Show Business*, *White Christmas*, and *Gentlemen Prefer Blondes*. The international facet of his film career has taken him to England, Italy, France, and Japan. In London he acted for a year in the stage smash *The Passion of Dracula* and starred in the BBC's "Notorious Woman," playing

Frédéric Chopin. He has appeared on numerous television shows and continues to perform in all areas of the entertainment field.

He noted: "What I love about dinner theatre is that you're right there—it's stimulating because it's immediate. You never know what to expect. It keeps you on your toes. I feel that I'm utilizing myself as a whole performer." When comparing his past dinner theatre work to his television and film experiences, Chakiris remarked: "It's great to feel the immediate feedback from the audience, whereas film work has little of that type of response. For me, performing for live audiences helps keep me in acting shape. My mind is working from beginning to end. In film, there is often a loss of continuity, shooting scenes out of order. My dinner theatre work has fine-tuned me for whatever comes next." When asked if he plans to do more dinner theatre, Chakiris responded: "Absolutely! I love doing live theatre. When I was first asked to perform at the Carousel, I didn't even have to think about it. I'm ready for more dinner theatre."

MONICA WEMITT, Actress, New York City

In the entertainment business for 22 years and acting professionally for 14 years, Monica Wemitt explained: "Dinner theatre is a very lucrative venue for actors at this point. The money is good and it's great to be able to work with such fine professionals. It ranks right under doing Broadway and nationals [tours]." She went on to say, "The audiences of dinner theatre are calmer audiences. They have time to sit, drink, eat, and enjoy. They're ready for a good time." In her own comical tone she compared it to New York. "In the city, you're fighting traffic for an hour trying to get to the theatre on time. When you get there you're ready to kill the cab driver. Dinner theatre is a more relaxed atmosphere, but the professionalism still comes out." Wemitt also points out one of the hazards of dinner theatre work for the actor: "It can be difficult when you're getting into character—thinking about your part and what you'll be doing—and then you get a whiff of fillet of sole and you start drooling. That can break your concentration." Wemitt wants to continue to do live theatre. She says it is a joy to try to convince audience members at every show that her performance for them is her "first."

Wemitt has seen a variety of changes over the past 14 years while working in dinner theatres across the country. And the changes have been for the better. She said: "The dinner theatres that are adapting to changes now will be the survivors. I feel they have to strive toward getting the younger audiences away from videos and television and into the theatre."

CINDY LAMB, Public Relations, Derby Dinner Playhouse, Clarksville, IN

Having handled public relations, advertising, and marketing for 15 years at the non-Equity 590-seat Derby Dinner Playhouse, Cindy Lamb feels there should be greater focus on getting the 25-to-34 age group to attend dinner theatre. Lamb stated: "This age bracket has limited disposable income and it will take educating them to increase their patronage." She explained that the bulk of those patrons over the age of 55 are often afraid to go out at night; thus the reason for plentiful attendance at the matinees. She says, "Our patronage from the 25-to-34 age bracket is equal to [that from] our 60-plus age bracket. It's a market we are developing."

What can be done to improve the general image of dinner theatre across the country? Lamb responds: "First of all, you must believe in your product in order to sell it. Then you must always be alert to the needs of the audience. We have comment cards that we collect from our patrons which help us to make all types of decisions. The managers meet once per month to review the comment cards. A good dinner theatre will listen to patrons. It's so important to know what they want." Another aspect that Lamb emphasizes is hospitality: "Each of our patrons feels like part of our family. Our season ticket holders who come regularly are known by name. It's a very friendly atmosphere. Our guests need to feel comfortable at our theatre and they need to know that they are welcome and important."

Another of Lamb's techniques in dealing with the public is her viewing of the operation from another perspective: "I think of our dinner theatre in other terms—we are a service organization, not just a dinner theatre. We receive all types of requests from schools, charities, community organizations and events, as well as from patrons. We extend ourselves to them as being 'their place.' The public relations and business value of this way of thinking is invaluable. We like to help them, and in turn they help us."

TOD KENT, Actor, New York City

"Dinner theatre has allowed me to be able to work with some top Broadway pros. I've learned so much by watching them and having the opportunity to work with these seasoned professionals. If I had remained in New York to take my chances, the roles would be smaller. But in the dinner theatre circuit I can perform more challenging roles that I ordinarily may not get."

Dinner theatre was ranked as the fifth largest employer (on a work-week basis) of professional stage actors in the United States in 1989, according to Actors' Equity Association. Times are tougher for younger actors and the competition today is stiffer. However, dinner theatre is a viable method for younger performers across the country to begin an acting career. Kent said, "At first I didn't know what to expect by doing dinner theatre, but it's great. The audiences can be more laid back at times, but every audience is different and unique."

Commenting on dinner theatre in the 1990s, Kent said: "It seems necessary to try to culturally stimulate our younger people toward live theatre. Theatre etiquette [i.e., applauding at the appropriate times, what to do and not do, etc.] is lacking from the younger audiences. This may be attributed to more of our youth attending movies and watching home videos. It's their parents and grandparents who grew up with live theatre."

One suggestion Kent made involves aiming musical presentations at younger audiences. He advises: "It seems that younger audiences are more issue oriented than one generation past. Issues that are thought provoking and controversial may be of more interest, as opposed to presenting another rendition of *Oklahoma!*." Having performed professionally now for over five years, but with a total of twelve years' experience under his belt, Kent feels that eventually he'd like to venture into movies and television as a way of both expanding his abilities and providing the exposure to allow him to do stage work in the future. He says, "Business-wise, I'd like to open all doors within the field, striving toward financial security as well as artistic fulfillment."

VIRGINIA KANCLER, Group Sales, Carousel Dinner Theatre, Akron

One of the key areas of any dinner theatre is the group sales division. And one of the bubbliest, not to mention most successful and knowledge-able individuals in the business, is Virginia Kancler.

She notes: "Team effort is one of the most important aspects of this business. You can get a group to come once, but if everything isn't perfect and their memories aren't positive, your groups will slowly drop off. Repeat business is very important. Once the patrons enter the lobby, they must be met with a smiling face—from the box office to the serving staff. Hospitality is a key to success. I meet them the moment they step off the bus. And it's great that the owner meets them as well. Everyone must work together in order for all parts of the picture to fit together."

Kancler takes bookings for over 1,600 groups at the (Equity-affiliated) Carousel during the year. These represent about 70,000 individuals from church groups, schools, organizations, corporations, and various tour operators. Kancler believes that "it's more than picking up the phone and booking groups." A group sales director must get out of the office in order to develop business, she says. Ontario Motorcoach, the National Tour

Association, and the American Bus Association have shows/conventions, as do numerous other tour operators; Kancler attends such events each year to increase the group business for her theatre.

Kancler, a person-oriented, meticulous workaholic, loves her job, her boss, and her facility. "I'm the lucky one," she exudes, "because my boss, Scott Griffith, is one of the best in the business. He's a mastermind because he knows this business. He's sharp as a tack and cares about each guest. That's exactly what I need for each patron to feel—from when they enter the Carousel to the time they re-board the bus. I love what I do! I guess I just have a lot of energy."

Networking is essential, according to Kancler, in order to develop group business. "We depend on other facilities just as they depend on us. I work with people all over the country. The tour operators provide us with guests and we entertain them with the magic of Broadway. . . . It's building rapport with people since this is totally a people business." One-, two-, and three-day tour packages Kancler has been coordinating for years. She said that such packages will become more and more necessary for dinner theatres throughout the 1990s. She noted: "Thinking ahead—months, even years is important when you're working with group leaders and tour operators. One needs to be creative when coming up with tour packages. The sky's the limit."

BOB STONE, Former Director of Food Services, Alhambra Dinner Theatre, Jacksonville, FL

"It's important that a food service director looks carefully at the market to determine what food items and food service type are most appropriate," says Bob Stone, past food service director and general operations manager of the (Equity-affiliated) Alhambra Dinner Theatre. Stone also has the distinction of being the president of the Restaurant Association's Northeast Florida chapter. "Quality and quantity are what our patrons have come to expect," explains Stone. "In our market the buffet works very well." The average age range for patrons attending the 406-seat dinner theatre is the mid-40s, according to Stone. "One thing that we are finding is a prevalent trend in most dinner theatres toward more health-oriented foods."

Stone was with the Alhambra for seven years, but has been in the food service industry for seventeen years. Trendwise, he feels that "healthier foods are becoming increasingly important to patrons. 'Healthy' refer to less salt, lower cholesterol, reduced fat, fresh fruits, and more special dietary requests from patrons."

Lowering the salt levels is the first step. He says that "cooks from the old school prepare foods with large quantities of salt. It's a matter of re-educating them to utilize more spices in lieu of salt." More patrons are asking for items like plain tuna, fresh fruits, plain chicken, and Kosher meals, but the main staples of the buffet will probably remain on the menu. He notes, "We present a beef dish, a chicken dish, and a seafood Newburg in our buffet. We provide two-to-three vegetables, five cold salad items, and four dessert selections." Since sauces help in keeping buffet food moist and appealing, it's important to be conscious of how the sauces are prepared and to make them as healthy as possible.

General industry trends, as Stone sees them, include more attention to the special needs of customers. Individual dietary requirements and special orders must be incorporated into a food service operation. Low sodium/ low cholesterol items in food selection and preparation must be given serious consideration.

Finally, the dining area (including buffet lines) must always be clean and attractive. Thus the goal of quality and quantity can still be achieved by dinner theatres across the country.

JOSEPH PATTON, Director and Choreographer, New York City

When Joseph Patton began directing and choreographing about 27 years ago, the climate was somewhat different. He explains: *"George M!, Hello, Dolly!,* and *Fiddler on the Roof* all opened and became available to theatres the same summer. *Sweet Charity, Man of La Mancha, Hello, Dolly!, On a Clear Day You Can See Forever,* and *Mame* were all playing on Broadway. Today it's different. That type of product, and in that quantity, is just not being produced." Although Patton also directs and choreographs for regional and summer stock theatres, a great deal of his time is spent on dinner theatre productions. He has worked for the Carousel Dinner Theatre, the Coachlight Dinner Theatre, the Drury Lane Dinner Theatre in Evergreen Park, Illinois, and Connecticut's Broadway Theatre. Patton comments on dinner theatre in the 1990s: "You can't just 'do' shows anymore. They must be done exceptionally well, using excellent designers, musicians, and actors. Because of competition and lack of product, patrons today must continue to perceive dinner theatre as a quality evening at a great bargain." Patton emphasized that in working closely with producers, he understands the necessity of budgets: "Dinner theatres are for-profit businesses, never funded by private or public arts institutions. John Kenley once said that you can spend a dime, but you better make it look like a dollar to the audience." Patton said that a show must look lavish but a producer needn't spend lavishly. He admitted costs have risen considerably over the past 27 years: "Broadway tickets were $9.90 or less back then. Today most theatres, including dinner theatres, are experiencing financial constraints. The producers who realize that they must make their product better, so that it becomes more attractive, will be the winners. For example, I frequently work with producers in negotiating for New York talent. I must always work within the producer's financial ranges, but the quality is out there and I do my best to find it."

Audiences today are more sophisticated, according to Patton. He notes: "Patrons have seen the big shows before, like *Oklahoma!*. What will bring them back? High-caliber productions, creative presentations, and a recognizable bargain. Theatre is an event, not like 'let's go to the movies.' It's something that's planned in advance. People may not always know what's bad, but it's human nature to know what's wonderful. Producers also need to develop interesting and clear marketing plans and maintain high standards throughout the entire operation in order for it to survive and grow through the 1990s."

Why is our theatre climate so different today as compared to several decades ago? Patton recalled: "During the 1950s and 1960s, show tunes were on the radio pop charts. Broadway actors would perform on the 'Ed Sullivan Show' and the 'Johnny Carson Show' and the musicals would become familiar to the public. This doesn't happen today. The last blockbuster family musical to be released that people knew about beforehand was *Annie*. That was in the early eighties."

Having directed, choreographed, and done casting for hundreds of shows, nationally and internationally, Patton feels that the type of show audiences enjoy most is about what people think and feel; about love, emotions, and relationships. That type of show, he thinks, makes a classic, and will continue to flourish on the dinner theatre circuit and in other areas of theatre. He added, "Dinner theatre customers must perceive a bargain, but yet they must receive quality all the way around."

PETER GRIGSBY, Former Director of Theatre Marketing, Marriott's Lincolnshire Theatre, Lincolnshire, IL

Marriott's Lincolnshire Theatre (Equity affiliated) is the only large corporately owned and produced theatre in the country. Peter Grigsby was at the helm of the theatre's marketing department for 13 years before deciding to leave in 1992 to pursue other interests. Grigsby predicts that the 1990s will lead dinner theatres toward innovative marketing techniques. He says, "While both strategy and operations are necessary for long-term success, it is the advantages of entrepreneurial thinking that will carry us into the next century."

Grigsby feels the audience is the key factor: "Without the excess baggage most non-profit theatres carry, such as reliance on federal or state funding and, in some cases, overblown artistic aspirations, dinner theatre entrepreneurs must respond directly to the wants and needs of their audience." Carefully considering facility space and the patrons needed to fill it, Grigsby said: "Our strategy for building our audience will become one of growth and replacement." Grigsby feels that new audiences must be cultivated for live theatrical entertainment (i.e., introducing children to live theatre) to counter the trend toward television and video tapes. He said that the industry must also recognize the utilization possibilities of performing spaces: children's theatre in the morning, the new "senior matinee" revues in the afternoon, main-stage performances in the evening, and concerts on dark nights.

"Given the current volatility of our economy, dinner theatres should reinforce their position as the best value in the competitive live-entertainment market. A national tour like *Miss Saigon*, reportedly asking $100 for choice seats, will position itself in the consumer's mind as a special event." When asked if this will hurt or help dinner theatres, Grigsby responded: "It will only serve to strengthen our 'one-stop-shopping' convenience of free parking, dinner, theatre, and, most importantly, value."

As Grigsby stated, a dinner theatre, possibly more than any other entertainment venue, is capable of responding (and must respond) to the nuances of local markets: "It is the audience orientation—the productions we present, the meals we serve, and the commitment to quality of service —that will impact our economic well-being in the 1990s."

MOVING FORWARD

It appears that the original concept of good food and quality live entertainment at a great price is still a fundamental tenet of the dinner theatre business. Getting an entertainment package for less than the price of purchasing the items individually may always be the main patron incentive contributing to this still-young industry.

After discussing what the future might hold for dinner theatre, those directly involved with the business said they see growth. In most cases, caution is the key thought—defined as being careful to "do it right." Even considering current changes within the food service industry and the entertainment field, the two are being melded effectively, and will continue to be, with proper management.

There probably is no magical formula that will guarantee success in this highly changeable business, however; if one reads between the lines, with good management and customer service, the bottom line may be expressed in mathematical terms: value + quality = success. This business formula may be the secret that owners and managers in the dinner theatre industry have known for years and will use throughout the 1990s.

CHAPTER 2

Historical Perspective

In determining where an industry is headed, it's also helpful to take a look at where it has been. The advent of an innovative concept, coupled with the "timbre of the times," produced fertile ground for the offer of dining and live performance as a package in one facility—known today as dinner theatre.

ROOTS

Dinner theatre is a relatively new concept. Its roots can be traced to the Hanover Tavern, outside Richmond, Virginia. In August 1953, David and Nancy Kilgore, along with four other actors, began using the tavern to present one-act plays and readings to the community. They then founded the Barksdale Theatre. To add to the evening's presentation, arrangements were made for certain groups to be served dinner in another room, prior to the play. Thus, in rough form, the foundations were laid for a new concept. Today, according to promotional literature, "Barksdale prefers to be known as a theatre that happens to have a restaurant, and dinner is optional." Nonetheless, that seed would develop into a concept that gradually grew into an international industry.

PULLINSI LIGHTS THE WAY

Six years later, in the summer of 1959, Bill Pullinsi, a first-year theatre student at Catholic University in Washington, D.C., started the Candlelight Theatre Restaurant in the city's Presidential Arms Hotel. His venture was actually the first dinner theatre since the 600 patrons had dinner and saw a show in the same room. Ironically, the term "theatre restaurant" now refers to an operation where dinner and a theatrical presentation are done in separate rooms; this is considered a subclassification of dinner theatre.

During Pullinsi's first season, his one-week presentations employed such stars as Pat O'Brien and Peggy Cass. During his second season in Washington, Pullinsi not only extended the runs to two weeks, but also pushed for a year-round season. He re-named his venture the Candlelight Dinner Playhouse. Because of the hotel's convention business, a year-round theatre operation was not possible. This gave Pullinsi the necessary incentive to return to his hometown of Chicago and to begin preparations for the nation's first 52-week dinner theatre, the Candlelight Dinner Playhouse. *Variety* ran several articles on this new concept and the theatrical press gave the opening a great deal of attention.

The original Candlelight, a converted roadside tavern owned by Pullinsi's grandfather, Bill Altier, seated 150 patrons. Then in 1964 a new building was constructed in Summit, Illinois, which seated 550 and retained table service for guests. Pullinsi's fellow student, Tony D'Angelo, designed and built most of the sets. Pullinsi's grandfather financed the operation and his mother, June, assisted at rehearsals. Today, Tony and June serve as associate producers.

MORE INNOVATIONS

The Candlelight was responsible for a number of arena stage innovations, including a hydraulic stage (which did not utilize cables or posts, resulting in no obstruction of sight lines), rolling stage wagons, flying scenery, and a mezzanine area that housed special lighting.

Today, Pullinsi's Candlelight Dinner Playhouse is one of four Equity dinner theatres in the Chicago area; the others are the Drury Lane Dinner Theatre, Drury Lane Theatre in Oakbrook Terrace, and Marriott's Lincolnshire Theatre. All subscribe to quality food service and high-caliber theatrical presentations.

In 1960, shortly after Pullinsi had opened his Illinois dinner theatre, the second dinner theatre emerged, in Cedar Grove, New Jersey. It was called the Meadowbrook Theatre Restaurant and had varied success. Its problems were attributed mainly to its size (over 700 seats with table-service dining), its proximity to Manhattan (only 23 miles away), and the expense of star attractions. Actors' Equity Association (the union representing stage actors) required Meadowbrook to pay Broadway production company minimums and operate under rules that added to their problems. In 1973 the operation closed.

In 1964, due west of Chicago, Carl Stohn opened the first dinner theatre run on the star system. His operation, called the Pheasant Run Dinner Theatre, was in St. Charles, Illinois. Over the years the business changed hands and format; currently it is not a dinner theatre. Stohn also ran the Drury Lane Dinner Theatre in Evergreen Park as a star house. Opening in 1952, it was built by Anthony DeSantis. DeSantis currently owns the Drury Lane in Oakbrook Terrace.

A PIONEER

One of the most influential men in the early development of the dinner theatre industry was Howard Wolfe of Virginia. Perhaps it began almost by accident, but from 1963 to 1970, Wolfe opened over a dozen dinner theatres across the country.

Several individuals who worked for the Barksdale Dinner Theatre in Hanover, Virginia, opened the Wedgewood Dinner Theatre in Williamsburg, Virginia, in the summer of 1963. Paul and Claudine Iddings, Charles Bush, Carolee Silcox, and Sandra Wade rented space in an old fish cannery and converted it into the Wedgewood. The theatre's building was owned by Howard Wolfe, the food manager was Charles Dorsey, and the operation was seasonal.

Being intrigued by this new type of business, Wolfe was inspired to open his first dinner theatre (with 220 seats) in Richmond, Virginia, on November 29, 1963. This dinner theatre was built from the ground up and included an elevator stage. It was operated by cables and posts and was termed the "magic stage" by Wolfe. John Pritchard and Doug Roberts worked for Wolfe at this operation. He named it The Barn, which was the beginning of what was considered a chain of similar dinner theatres across the country.

With partners Connelly Jones and Dr. Ernest Spanger, Howard Wolfe built the second Barn Dinner Theatre, in Greensboro, North Carolina, in 1964. The design was similar to that of the first and it seated 350 patrons. Soon after, Barn number three was constructed in Atlanta, Georgia, in 1965 by Wolfe and Jones.

THE BARNS FLOURISH

Howard Wolfe went on to build Barn Dinner Theatres in other cities with the assistance of Asberry Chaffin and his son John, both of Nashville,

Tennessee. Wolfe's Barns went up in Roanoke, Virginia, in 1965; in Norfolk, Virginia, in 1966; in Winchester, Kentucky, in 1966; in Kingsport, Tennessee, in 1966; in Knoxville, Tennessee, in 1966; in Morrisville, North Carolina, in 1966; in Marietta, Georgia, in 1966; in Matthews, North Carolina, in 1967; in Nashville, in 1967; in Charlotte, North Carolina, in 1967; in Tampa, Florida, in 1968; in Houston, Texas, in 1968; in Albuquerque, New Mexico, in 19688; in Dallas, Texas, in 1968; in Columbus, Ohio, in 1969; in Jackson, Mississippi, in 1969; and in Huntington, West Virginia, in 1970. But these were begun without the help of Charles Dorsey, Doug Roberts, and John Pritchard, who broke away from Wolfe and Company to begin their own dinner theatre operation outside Baltimore, Maryland.

Indeed, with backing from Garland Henning and Richard Hamlin, the Beaver Dam Dinner Theatre was begun in Cockeysville, Maryland, in 1965, under the leadership of Dorsey, Roberts, and Pritchard. It was opened in a ski lodge and continued operating until the ski season in November of that year. The dinner theatre was then temporarily closed until the summer of 1966, when it was re-named the Oregon Ridge Dinner Theatre and opened in a building erected next to the ski lodge expressly for this purpose. It was run as an Equity theatre until 1979 and is now operated on weekends under a non-profit status. Bobbie Baker's Carousel Dinner Theatre opened in 1967 in Ocean Park, Maryland, but only survived for one summer season. In 1969, Hamlin and Henning opened the Garland Dinner Theatre in Columbia, Maryland, which was also an Equity theatre until 1979. It still operates, as Toby's Dinner Theatre. Also influenced by the Oregon Ridge operation were the Bolton Hill Dinner Theatre and the Limestone Valley Dinner Theatre in Cockeysville, Maryland, begun by Hamlin and Henning in 1969.

A DINNER THEATRE FRANCHISE

Eventually the Barns became a franchised business. Wolfe formed and owned a New York City production company called Theatre Productions International, which would travel to each of the franchises. Each franchisee owned one-twenty-fifth of the company. However, during 1970–71 Wolfe filed a number of lawsuits against franchise operators in a dispute over franchise fees. Within this two-year period the lawsuits were settled and the franchises were dissolved. As a result, some of the owners received money, others paid Wolfe money, and yet other owners got nothing. Names of the dinner theatres were changed and owners went their separate ways. Wolfe still owned a number of dinner theatres and also began another theatre group, in Tennessee, Florida, and Texas, called the Holiday Dinner Theatres. This group was to be affiliated with the Holiday Inn chain, but a lawsuit immediately ensued and the association never came to fruition.

A SOUTHWESTERN CHAIN

In the Southwest, another chain of dinner theatres, known as the Windmill Dinner Theatres, was started by Tom Eisner in 1967 and these were heavily influenced by Wolfe's Barn in Dallas. The first Windmill was in fact Wolfe's Barn in Dallas, and then others began operating in Fort Worth, Texas; Scottsdale, Arizona; and Houston. Don Crute opened the Country Dinner Playhouse in Dallas and assisted Bob Boren and Sam Newton with the design for their operation of the same name in Denver. Bill McHale, who then worked for Crute, directed shows at the Country Dinner Playhouses in Dallas and Denver. Crute's other Country Dinner Playhouses (under the name Dinner Theatres, Inc.) were in Columbus, Ohio; San Antonio, Texas; and St. Petersburg, Florida. After Boren and Newton built the Country Dinner Playhouse in Denver in 1970, Eisner sold them the Windmill chain. The Derby Dinner Playhouse in Clarksville, Indiana, was also built by Boren and Newton, and the Crystal Palace in Dallas was acquired by them and turned into a Windmill Dinner Theatre. No professional dinner theatres exist in Texas today.

Gerald Moss and Howard Wolfe built the Barn Dinner Theatre in St. Louis, Missouri, which was followed in that city by the Curtain Up Dinner Theatre and the Plantation in 1974, and then by the Magic Stage Dinner Theatre.

OTHERS BEGIN

It seemed that dinner theatres were springing up just about everywhere during the mid-sixties and early seventies. Dow Sherwood started the Showboat Dinner Theatres, first in Greensboro, North Carolina, in 1966, and then in Clearwater, Florida, in 1967. Nate Block and Joe Ryan began the Westroads Dinner Theatre in Omaha, Nebraska, which was a spin-off of the In-The-Round Dinner Theatre in Chicago. The Gaslight Dinner Theatre chain was started by Doug Condley in 1968 with an operation in Tulsa; then, the following year, a theatre in Oklahoma City; and, finally, one in Memphis, Tennessee, in 1970. Other spin-offs of the Westroads were the Firehouse Dinner Theatre and the Talk of the Town Dinner Theatre, which both opened in Omaha in 1973. Herbert and Carol

Bloomberg founded the Chanhassen Theatres in Chanhassen, Minnesota, a complex that eventually included four theatres that were purchased by the International Broadcasting Corporation in 1989.

Another individual in the construction field who built dinner theatres was Scott Talbott. He built the first Beef 'N Boards Dinner Theatre, in Simpsonville, Kentucky, in 1967. The second Beef 'N Boards was constructed in Harrison, Ohio (near Cincinnati), and the third was built in Indianapolis, Indiana, in 1973. Don Crute's company, DTI (Dinner Theatres, Inc.), bought the Indianapolis and Harrison operations from Talbott. In 1978 Bob Zehr and Doug Stark struck up a deal, while at dinner with Talbott, to buy the Simpsonville Beef 'N Boards. Because financial troubles were causing DTI to crumble, it sold Zehr and Stark its remaining two Beef 'N Boards theatres. The Harrison facility operated for another two years, but was not profit generating and was closed in 1982. Zehr and Stark still own the only remaining Beef 'N Boards Dinner Theatre, in Indianapolis.

In nearby Ohio, David Fulford began the Carousel Dinner Theatre in 1973, in a converted grocery store in Ravenna. It was an arena theatre, with buffet food service, that seated 512. In 1978 the dinner theatre was plagued with financial woes, and Prescott F. Griffith came in from New York to manage the operation. Griffith completed a full buyout of the theatre from Fulford in December 1986. Griffith moved his operation to a newly created 1,130-seat facility in Akron, Ohio—making it the largest dinner theatre anywhere in the country.

SOUTHEASTERN THEATRES

While Wolfe's franchised Barn Dinner Theatres were proving successful, numerous independents were springing up throughout the Southeast. North Carolina became home in 1965 to the Pineville Dinner Theatre in Pineville, owned by Bill Lorick, Sr., and operated by Bill Hartigan from 1974 until its closing in 1981. The Village Dinner Theatre in Morrisville (1965–81) was originally a Wolfe operation but was purchased by Hal Payne in 1967 and subsequently bought by Hartigan in June 1968. Other operations included Charlie Brown's Lakeside in Raleigh (1985–86); the Showboat Dinner Theatre in Greensboro (1967–71); and the Off-Broadway Dinner Theatre in Charlotte (1974–75).

South Carolina had the Country Dinner Theatre in Pelham (1967–70), owned by several investors during its three-year existence and operated by Hartigan. Also, the Columbia Dinner Theatre, located in Columbia (1969–70), had only a one-year life.

In Tennessee a chain known as the Old West Dinner Theatres was opened by Paul Barker, with a theatre in Kingsport (1966); one in Chattanooga (1967–73, and then reopened, 1977–80); and finally, the third, in Memphis (1967–71), which was later taken over by the Gaslight Dinner Theatre (1971–80). The Hurricane Dinner Playhouse in Hurricane, West Virginia, was an independent that began in 1964 and is still operating. Virginia also adopted the dinner theatre concept, with the opening of the Cavalier Dinner Theatre in Norfolk (1966–74), an original Wolfe operation; the Lazy Susan Dinner Theatre in Springfield, which changed owners many times; the Hayloft Dinner Theatre in Manassas (1971–90); and the Tidewater Dinner Theatre in Portsmouth (1971–   ).

Going further south, the Derby Dinner Playhouse in Hot Springs, Arkansas (1967), had only two productions before turning into a nightclub. Murry's Dinner Playhouse, started by the late Ike Murry, began in September 1967 and is still in operation in Little Rock.

In Atlanta, the Tally-Ho Dinner Theatre (1966–71) was opened through a consortium of investors, was originally an Equity theatre, and operated by Bill Hartigan. The Atlanta Dinner Theatre (1966–70) was owned by Milos Hanza and produced its own shows. Hanza also created the Beverly Dinner Playhouse in Covington, Kentucky (1968–69). In the 1970s, two more dinner theatres opened in Atlanta, the Mid-Nite Sun, originally an Equity theatre (1973–75); and the Hayloft Dinner Theatre (1976–77), which reportedly had a $500,000 operating loss.

Aside from the Florida chains, independents opened, including the Orange Blossom Playhouse in Orlando, Florida, which was eventually converted into a nightclub (1966–68); Vince Parrenti's Country Dinner Playhouse in Fort Lauderdale, which also was turned into a nightclub shortly after the owner's death (1967–68); and the Sea Ranch Dinner Theatre in Fort Lauderdale, owned by Brian Smith and opened in 1974.

OTHER VENUES

There were three dinner theatres in Kansas City, Missouri. Two of them were owned by Dinner Playhouses, Inc., Tiffany's Attic and Waldo Astoria. The founders of DPI, Dennis Hennessy and Richard Carrothers, are still co-owners of the operation. Waldo Astoria closed in 1991. The third, owned by the late James Assad, was called the American Heartland Theatre. Both Equity affiliated they began operations in the early 1970s.

In July 1974, William Stutler and Robert Funking began An Evening Dinner Theatre in Elmsford, New York, and it has continued to operate under an Equity contract. An Evening Dinner Theatre was moved down the street from the previous location to a newly constructed building. The name was changed to the Westchester Broadway Theatre. The only professional year-round Equity theatre in Connecticut is the Darien Dinner Theatre, which recently changed its name to Connecticut's Broadway Theatre. The operation was begun in 1977 and it changed ownership in 1983. Jane Bergere became the executive producer and chief operating officer in 1985.

RECENT CHANGES

Recently, there have been numerous changes taking place in the dinner theatre industry, and most have been very positive ones.

Today, as was the case in the 1960s, buildings are being constructed; new operations are opening; locations have been changed to finer facilities; second theatres are springing up in some places; expansions are being planned; and artists' renderings sit before investors.

Why are there so many changes? Perhaps they are reactions to the market. Well-established dinner theatres, such as the Carousel in Akron, have moved into elegant and spacious buildings. The trend is to expand toward full-service entertainment facilities. One theatre, the Ascot in Denver, has beaten the odds and built a completely new facility.

A NEW DYNASTY IN DENVER

So far, it hasn't been particularly smooth sailing for Mark Turpin, executive producer and managing general partner involved in creating the Ascot Dinner Theatre in Denver, Colorado. Turpin discussed how and why he became executive producer: "I got stuck with it. I was a general partner in this and was involved in a very minor way. And then our previous managing general partner obviously didn't quite have things under control. So I decided, 'Well, I'll just come back here and use my technical expertise and help out.' So I wound up getting slid in as a technical director. And then she [the managing general partner] disappeared. It turned out she'd embezzled $700,000 from the business and left us high and dry!

"I was the only one who knew what was going on—who sort of had the big picture of where things were. We were 20 percent done with construction when she left us with several hundred thousand dollars' worth of construction contracts hanging loose, and no money to pay them; and two and one-half million dollars' worth of loans sitting out here with no money to pay them. It took about a year for me to reassemble the pieces. We went out and pounded the pavement and we were finally able to fund this with some bank financing and some additional capital from the general partnership. That's why, to be perfectly honest, I sort of backed into it. But, it was either that or it wasn't going to happen."

Like a story line from a night-time soap opera, this unexpected shift in management may have given the Ascot a more solidified focus. Turpin says, "What we're providing, the thing that we're focusing on, is the total experience." A producer or theatre owner's dream, according to Turpin, is an audience that will decide to come to the theatre for the overall experience, and not primarily because of what show is playing.

Located in a high-density, white-collar, suburban Denver area, the Ascot occupies 30,000 square feet. With a degree in engineering, Turpin has played an integral role in the theatre's design and development. The Ascot is a non-Equity house that opened with *My Fair Lady* in March 1990.

Looking back over the years since its opening, Turpin reflected: "As far as dinner service and theatrical product go, we are today amazingly close to what we set out to do." Turpin feels it is a major accomplishment. Although the theatre is a beautiful and tasteful facility, appropriate for the type of elegant total experience his clientele expect, the Ascot was 10–20 percent below the projected ticket sales for the first year, and obviously that hurt financially.

Over 80,000 patrons passed through the Ascot's doors during the last three quarters of 1990. Since customer service was considered to be of prime importance, comment cards were carefully analyzed for suggestions to change elements of the operation that needed alteration, or to add or delete elements. That, according to Turpin, has been an ongoing process from day one and may account for the overwhelmingly positive patron response. With regard to the shows, he explained that reviews of the first few shows were not as good as they had hoped, but production problems are being ironed out, as are difficulties in the food and service areas. In light of these improvements, Turpin is sorry that he could not have increased his sales during his first year to achieve a breakeven status. All in all, not bad for an individual starting from scratch and beginning to realize a dream in what is considered by most to be a difficult industry.

Turpin is proud of the fact that he maintains black-tie waiter service, linen tablecloths, and chandelier-laden interiors, providing a classy ambiance within his 700-seat facility. Turpin has so far accomplished creating a dinner theatre from the ground up during a turbulent economic period. Through his insight, he has been able to promote the total experience for all of his patrons.

DOWN THE ROAD

Most dinner theatre owners think about adapting their operations to present conditions. However, William Stutler and Robert Funking, co-owners of the Westchester Broadway Theatre in Elmsford, New York, have already begun preparing for the twenty-first century.

Their plans do not include redecorating the walls or changing the flatware. Instead, they had envisioned and indeed created a new $4.5 million structure that now will better serve those who have supported the 400-seat dinner theatre since 1974, and those who will experience it for the first time. Not only was a new building created, but a new name as well; the Westchester Broadway Theatre will carry on the tradition begun by An Evening Dinner Theatre in 1974.

An Evening Dinner Theatre had been chosen then as the operation's name to convey a concept in entertainment—the total experience of professional theatre and fine dining under one roof, and at a reasonable price. Tickets for dinner and show range from $27 to $45, and only a small increase is projected. In effect, Stutler and Funking feel that they have now firmly established this concept in their market.

The Westchester Broadway Theatre, located only one block from the old theatre, reflects what Stutler and Funking feel is the essence of their business: a permanent professional Equity theatre where Broadway performers, directors, and designers gather to create Broadway entertainment.

Stutler and Funking are not new to the dinner theatre business. *Who's Who* says, in part: "Messrs. Funking and Stutler have produced more shows than most established Broadway producers. *Anything Goes* marks their 82nd full-length Broadway show. An Evening is the longest running, 52-week-a-year Equity theatre in New York State."

One might think that by doubling the square footage to 32,000, some degree of intimacy would be lost. Not so, say the producers. Even though the square footage has in fact increased, only 49 seats were added to the theatre. Guests can still enjoy the intimacy that the three-quarter thrust stage design offers. Most of the additional space has been allocated to production, food service, the box office, and the group sales area.

Perhaps one of the nicer extras is the use of four celebrity boxes that provide fine dining and private viewing of the show for parties of six or more. Also part of this "ring of elegance" formed along the upper tier are private powder-room facilities, coat closets, and a cordial bar. A special team of waiters is reserved only for the boxes.

But all guests can enjoy the two-story atrium window surrounding the theatre entrance. Ribbons of fabric billow over the lobby. A special stairway leads patrons to the celebrity boxes. All in all, the producers have created a fresh and exciting theatre facility that patrons will enjoy and perhaps marvel at time and again.

Stutler and Funking took a risk by moving their facility and investing additional capital in what can be considered a somewhat new venture. But their eyes were toward the future. They've laid their foundations. During 819 weeks of continuous operation, they've served over 2 million patrons, employed over 2,000 professional actors and musicians, and aided the fund-raising efforts of over 5,000 charities. It seems that they've done it correctly. The Westchester Broadway Theatre will bring into realization the quality changes that Stutler and Funking feel are necessary for the future.

THOUGHTFUL CHANGE

In spite of the constant economic shifts over the past several years, it is apparent that growth is still occurring in the dinner theatre industry. What's more, it seems that those theatres that adapt to changes in their respective markets will become the top dogs. The barometer of change indicates market savvy for the 1990s. As evidenced by the newly created Ascot, the relocated Westchester Broadway, and other dinner theatres, the quality of dining, service, and the show throughout the industry has improved. More full-service entertainment operations are emerging with lavish and well-planned seasons, with stars in the sky and on the stage. Most of the successful dinner theatres are no longer ma-and-pa weekend theatres, but have naturally developed into full-time, professional operations. Change is an inevitable factor, but one that must be dealt with effectively by every dinner theatre, lest they become victims of the memories of the past.

BRINGING THE PRESENT INTO FOCUS

With today's economic hardships, most dinner theatres would agree that the overall stability of the industry is being threatened. Cost-saving measures and new promotional ideas are paramount if theatres are to expand, let alone remain in business. It certainly is a challenge of the times. But those dinner theatres who meet this challenge with creative, yet effective means will end up the winners.

In the recent past, both the Darien Dinner Theatre and An Evening Dinner Theatre changed their names to better suit their market and image. The Candlelight Dinner Playhouse re-dedicated its Forum Theatre for a comedy series—a logical use of existing space. Jan McArt opened her

Upstairs Cabaret Room at the Royal Palm Dinner Theatre in Boca Raton, Florida, and opened her International Room at the Marco Polo Resort in Miami Beach. Other dinner theatres across the country utilized space more carefully, and conserved and cut back in all areas to become more efficient.

Not all survived, however. For example, the Union Plaza Dinner Theatre closed its doors in Las Vegas, as did the Waldo Astoria in Kansas City, Missouri.

In 1991 the American Dinner Theatre Institute and Actors' Equity Association battled at the bargaining table in negotiations lasting over five months. They agreed on a contract after acknowledging the economic hardships befalling the industry's Equity-affiliated dinner theatres. Keys to molding an amicable agreement were the ADTI personnel on their negotiating team, including Scott Griffith, president; Jane Bergere, first vice president; Kary Walker, second vice president; Jim Jude, treasurer; Virginia Sherwood, secretary; and William Lynk, executive director. The Society of Stage Directors and Choreographers also recognized the economic problems during their contract talks with ADTI during the autumn of 1991.

To counteract the problems of the times, the Showboat Dinner Theatre produced shows never done before, to create excitement and draw a new market to the theatre. Golden Apple Dinner Theatres did some of the war-horses on overseas tours. Chanhassen Dinner Theatres revived *Me and My Girl* later in the same year they first presented it. The Drury Lane Oakbrook Theatre delighted audiences with *The Phantom of the Opera*, the best audience reception ever in 41 years!

With the heyday of summer stock gone, dinner theatre has become the proving ground for many aspiring Broadway actors. The Carousel in Akron, for example, had 35 of its past performers appearing in Broadway shows during the month of July in 1991. Indeed, an old image of dinner theatre is slowly being shed and its value and prominence are blossoming.

Bob Funking, co-owner of the Westchester Broadway Theatre, just north of New York City, is cautiously optimistic about what the future will bring: "Dinner theatre offers value—great value, comparably speaking." Funking pointed out that patrons realize the enormous value inherent in the dinner and the show ticket, as opposed to paying for a show elsewhere and dinner at a restaurant. But even though people will always go out, they are tending to go out less. This translates into less repeat business. He said: "If our patrons usually attend four shows, they may now only come to two. They may have come to a comedy night or a special performance two weeks later, whereas now they may not." This change is felt to be a direct result of the economic slump that pervades the country.

weeks later, whereas now they may not." This change is felt to be a direct result of the economic slump that pervades the country.

He noted: "The middle class is our largest market segment—including skilled blue-collar workers. Many of them work in the construction trades and are unemployed at this point and that hurts us all, as well as the economy." Perceptively, Funking sees the long-range answer as a national measure: stimulating the economy. He pointed out that a drop in interest rates helped slightly, but he said employment must be boosted. He said that short-term solutions include creative marketing and access to new products.

"Obtaining [a] new product is very helpful, but it's hard to get. Especially here, so close to New York City. To generate interest in our recent production of *Sugar*, a musical that is not well known, we ran the movie *Some Like It Hot*, on which it is based, on a TV monitor in our lobby before the show opened. People are familiar with the movie and it helped sales." This is one successful example of creativity mixed with marketing. Also mentioned was a "tightening of the money belt." Funking said that he is going to push more with television advertising even though it's rather expensive in the New York market. Westchester's sale for January to June of 1992 are down as compared to the same time during 1991, but because he has been more careful with expenses and controlling production costs, he feels the future will be brighter for New York's only Equity-affiliated, year-round dinner theatre.

"A blockbuster year" is what Tony D'Angelo, co-owner of the first U.S. dinner theatre, the Candlelight Dinner Playhouse in Chicago, calls 1992. He says: "If they [his patrons] want to see a show, they'll buy a ticket. If they're not interested in the show, they won't. They seem to be more selective regarding what they'll see." He further defined his "blockbuster year" by saying that shows need to be well known by the public, if sales are to be brisk. The Candlelight produced *Evita!* and sales were excellent; however, a lesser-known musical, *Little Me*, was not very good for the Candlelight in a business sense.

D'Angelo expressed the same concern cited by Funking and by most other dinner theatre owners: the fact that new and exciting products, that is, new Broadway-type musicals, are not easy to come by. Patrons want to see new shows, but, at the same time, they are not willing to risk spending their hard-earned dollars on an unfamiliar production. It's like a Catch-22. If a show such as *Miss Saigon* were immediately available, it could very well sell out at many dinner theatres, not necessarily because the public knows what the musical is about, but because they are familiar with the title, through national publicity. Since dinner theatres do not have access to national grants and are not subsidized by other organizations, owners must be exceedingly careful when making their show-title choices for a season, or even when trying to predict what their audiences will choose to see. This, too, can be an extremely risky business decision.

Assuming that a show is one that audiences do want to see, a theatre must then be filled. Tod Booth, owner of the Alhambra Dinner Theatre, in Jacksonville, pointed out that his business has its ups and downs and tends to be dependent on the local economy, which was also influenced by the Persian Gulf War. He said: "We have four bases in Jacksonville with about 40,000 military personnel here, pumping about three billion dollars into our local economy. With many of these people away, it's created a definite impact on our area." Booth also indicated that the state of the national economy has had adverse effects on his operation. Furthermore, all of the four largest local banks recently lost millions due to bad debts. One bank, Booth stated, lost $29 million. Booth's plans to build a new theatre are temporarily frozen until economic conditions reverse themselves. He does, however, see things slowly changing for the better. Even though his current ticket sales and advance sales are down slightly, Booth hopes his choice of shows will attract a crowd made weary by money woes.

Clearly, dinner theatre is providing a value-oriented product to an increasingly value-minded public. With a lack of new titles for the dinner theatre circuit, owners and operators are tending to make do in the best way they can. Everything from the cost of napkins of employee salaries is being judiciously monitored to trim excesses. "Cost savings" is a term that seems to be a national catch-phrase. Thus if dinner theatres continue to adapt to the needs of the markets they serve, and, if they persevere in battling the economy, while maintaining the quality of food, entertainment, and service they've become known for, the future will be bright for the dinner theatre industry. In fact, at the start of the 1990s, there were approximately 100 dinner theatres in operation across the United States. Many of the earlier dinner theatres that had been created in the sixties and seventies were no longer functioning. Some had changed names and moved locations. New dinner theatres were still being created.

An awareness of the elaborate history of this industry, from the original concept to its implementation today, should give the reader a sense of awe and of deeper insight into its development. For those connected closely with it, hopefully the past may give clues as to the mistakes and successes of the industry's pioneers so that the mistakes will become lessons learned and will not be repeated.

CHAPTER 3

The "Dinner" in Dinner Theatre

PRESENTATION AND QUALITY

All too often, when reviewing dinner theatre, critics will gloss over, if not negate entirely, the dining experience. There are theatre critics and there are food critics. Each group reviews what it knows best. Possibly, neither wants to invade the other's turf. But what ends up happening in a dinner theatre review is a thorough critique of the show, with no mention of the meal or of the food service.

The elements of theatre and food are concomitant features in any successful dinner theatre business. From an elaborate buffet to elegant table service, the presentation and quality must go hand in hand.

THE BUFFET

According to John Chaffin, owner and operator of Chaffin's Barn in Nashville, there are two basics in a successful buffet; and these factors are not peculiar to any region or market. One factor is good food, and plenty of it. The second is the importance of having quality food at a reasonably low price.

Chaffin not only operates the Barn theatre, but also oversees all kitchen activities, from creating recipes and menus to ordering food. He works with the cooks, but is considered the chef. He has been doing this since 1963.

Certainly, regional differences occur in the putting together of a successful buffet. "A buffet I put together in Nashville just wouldn't work in

Birmingham," Chaffin said, "although there are some basic foods that seem to work just about anywhere." These include roast beef, mashed potatoes, and green beans. But was this always so? What about 25 years ago, when dinner theatres were blossoming?

1960s Mainstay

The mainstay of the dinner theatre food service in the early sixties was the buffet, with an emphasis on elegance. Chaffin described the decorative ice carvings and fresh flowers that surrounded the buffet. The time and expense involved were incredible. This trend toward the fancy has been replaced by more simplicity in some markets, with an emphasis on health-oriented foods. Patrons in Chaffin's market are aware that the visual extras will cost them more, and a price-conscious group will simply do without embellishments and prefer quality and quantity for the same (or a lower) price.

PRESENT TREND

In many markets the trend is toward table service. Today, many more individuals will buy the dinner theatre package for the total experience. Most couples are two wage earners who have worked all day and want to sit back in comfortable dinner theatre surroundings and be pampered, which includes being served, as opposed to waiting in a line for food. Quality entertainment should then follow. This type of thinking by patrons reflects changes in the work force and in the times; however, it does not reflect the attitude in all markets.

Marque Sandrock, director of operations at the Carousel Dinner Theatre in Akron, feels that table service can be very effective, depending on the type and size of the facility and on the economic level of the market concerned. He notes: "Successful buffets must rely on both quality and quantity, but the emphasis is clearly on quantity. With the ever-increasing demands for health-conscious entrees, plated service offers the operator the challenging opportunity to seriously concentrate on quality and presentation. This also allows the operator to establish a reputation as a fine dining establishment, thereby creating an additional selling point which the prospective guests will not overlook when deciding where to spend their evening." Sandrock feels that the producer's food costs related to table service can be the same as buffet costs, but the food quality is much better. He says: "The same per-person cost factors can be maintained in either service style, whereas the cost factor for a buffet is most affected by quantity. However, plated service allows the operator to focus that dollar cost on the quality of the product being presented."

Health-Conscious Patrons

The health kick of the late eighties has continued into the nineties. Food industry representatives feel that good nutrition awareness is no longer a trend but has led to a gradual change in eating habits for most people. And now it affects the purchase and preparation of food in the dinner theatre industry. Both Chaffin and Sandrock say that they prepare foods that are low in sodium, fat, and cholesterol. Chaffin claims that one-half of his buffet qualifies as part of this health-conscious effort. Sandrock also says that his full-service staff allows for greater flexibility in providing special orders for those guests with dietary requirements. But Sandrock added that most of his northeastern Ohio patrons are still interested in a "filling meal," and that the midwestern meat-and-potatoes dinner is still extremely popular.

The Little Extras

Sandrock and his chef, Lisa Johnston, have created a menu that caters to those desiring gourmet foods, such as lobster tails and filet mignon. Some of their other menu items include baked stuffed orange roughy with a light cream sauce, rack of lamb, medallions of veal, and chicken Wellington. The menu changes for each show (sample menus are shown at the end of this chapter. Sandrock and Johnston feel that with a good presentation of quality food, the general image of dinner theatre food will improve.

WILL IT EVER STAND OUT?

Most people would agree that, historically, dinner theatre food has not been comparable to food served in a four-star restaurant, the reason being that the dinner theatre experience is a blend of dinner and a show—a package. The experience consists of a hearty meal and top entertainment under one roof. In most cases, it's the show that is the main attraction, and the food is an extra incentive. John Chaffin said that "I would never exist as only a restaurant, nor would I exist as only a theatre—it's the package at a very reasonable price that sells the dinner theatre experience."

One must also consider budgets. Sandrock explained that the income status of the patrons and the socioeconomic level of the general market area will affect ticket prices and consequently what can be done with the food budget. He said: "People are realizing that a comparable show at a local playhouse will cost a patron $35 and dining out may cost $25. The dinner/show package for one will only cost $28.50. Obviously there is a significant savings here."

Dinner Theatre Reviewers

Perhaps most dinner theatres won't ever be rated as highly as a four-star restaurant, but the quality in most operations has greatly improved over the past 30 years. Theatre critics, of course, emphasize the show. Most do not mention the food or the related service. Sandrock feels that this is not necessarily bad since most theatre critics may not be sensitive to factors that experienced food critics would notice. On the other hand, food critics would need to be sensitive to budgetary restrictions imposed by the nature of the dinner theatre business.

OTHER FOOD AVENUES

Some dinner theatre operations are expanding their food service division outside the theatre. More outside parties are being catered along with inside banquets and other events. Since dinner theatres are moving toward a more educated management, these other avenues offer great income potential for the dinner theatre.

Specialty-drink glasses (with a theatre logo) and signature desserts in souvenir containers are other big sellers at the Carousel. Sandrock also said that they have sold as many as 4,000 specialty glasses in a 12-week period. An example of a signature dessert, created for the show *Little Shop of Horrors*, was a "Feed Me Mud Pie." This dessert blended layers of crushed Oreos and Heath Bars, chocolate cream, and fudge, served in a plastic souvenir flower pot complete with a bloom.

PLEASING EVERYONE ALL THE TIME?

It just can't be done, not when there are so many different needs, wants, and tastes related to people and to food service. If all these factors are kept in proper focus, dinner theatre food service will do what it set out to do: create the best possible dining experience for the theatre's patrons.

Obviously, there are trends that need to be considered. The use of extravagant visuals in food presentations depends on markets and times. However, both the country buffet and the gourmet table service menu must present food items in an appealing and appetizing manner.

Even though quantity and quality are still the norm, more individuals are gravitating toward health-conscious menus. It seems that people want enough food, but not too much. What they eat is of greater concern than just eating a lot.

The total experience is what dinner theatre promoters are encouraging, whether they offer a buffet or table service. The patron is enjoying the convenience of dinner and a show under one roof and for one low price. This package is what makes a dinner theatre different from any restaurant and different from any theatre.

For restaurant-related books of interest to the dinner theatre operator, see "Professional References" in Chapter 8.

American Musical Theatre and Dinner At Its Sensational Best!

Dining Selections

ACT ONE
Appetizers

(Available at an additional charge.)

ONION SOUP GRATINEE
Homemade onion soup prepared with three different types of onions, topped with a unique crouton and provolone cheese.................... $3.25

SOUP DU JOUR
Enjoy a cup of our freshly made soup. Ask your server for today's special.
... $2.25

SHRIMP COCKTAIL
Five large gulf shrimp served with our own cocktail sauce and crackers.
... $7.25

STUFFED MUSHROOM CAPS
Four large mushrooms stuffed with our chef's mixture of crab, mushrooms and herbs. $3.75

MOZZARELLA STICKS
Breaded mozzarella cheese sticks that are deep fried and served with our own cocktail sauce. $3.50

SHRIMP & CRAB AU GRATIN
Shrimp and crabmeat baked in a white sauce with mild cheese and garnished with parsley and lemon wheel. $6.75

FRESH VEGETABLE PLATTER (Serves Two)
Carrots, celery, cauliflower, broccoli, cucumbers, cherry peppers and olives served with a spinach cream cheese dip. $3.25

CHEESE BOARD
An assortment of domestic and international cheeses, grapes and Carousel's famous cheese ball. Served with crackers........................ $5.75

FRESH FRUIT PLATTER
Watermelon, cantaloupe, honeydew, strawberries and grapes served with our chef's secret Amaretto dip.   Full platter (Serves 3-6) $7.95
                                    Half platter (Serves Two) $4.50

HOT APPETIZER SAMPLER
An assortment of four broiled waterchestnuts glazed and wrapped in bacon, four breaded mozzarella cheese sticks and two large mushroom caps stuffed with a pleasing blend of crab, mushrooms and herbs. $4.95

Carousel Dinner Theatre. Akron, Ohio.

MAIN ATTRACTION
Entrees

PRIME RIB
Special house cut of prime rib topped with au jus and served with potato and seasonal vegetable.

Rare - Warm, red center
Medium - Hot, pink center
Well - Hot, thoroughly cooked

CHICKEN WELLINGTON
Boneless breast of chicken topped with a mushroom and onion duxelle then wrapped in puff pastry. Baked to perfection and served with wild rice and seasonal vegetables.

STUFFED ORANGE ROUGHY
Boneless orange roughy stuffed with crabmeat and bread crumbs. Baked and topped with a light cheese sauce. Served with wild rice and seasonal vegetable.

STEAMSHIP ROUND OF PORK
Slow roasted pork topped with a savory mushroom sauce. Served with potato and seasonal vegetable.

BACON & ZUCCHINI LASAGNA
Canadian bacon, zucchini and ricotta cheese wrapped in lasagna noodles. Baked and topped with our own Alfredo sauce. Served with a garlic breadstick.

Vegetarian Plate Available Upon Request.

Your Dinner and Show Ticket Price Includes
One Main Attraction Entree, Carousel Salad with choice of French, Italian,
Thousand Island, Blue Cheese, Ranch or Sweet and Sour Poppy Dressing,
Crumbled Blue Cheese (75¢ additional charge) and fresh rolls.
Maxwell House® *Coffee*, Sanka® *Decaffeinated Coffee* and Tea
prior to the performance.

INTERMEZZO
Desserts

Lush . . . lavish . . . and absolutely divine!
(Available at an additional charge.)

For better service we suggest that you pre-order your intermission desserts
before the start of the performance.

VANILLA ICE CREAM $1.50
        with chocolate sauce $1.75

SHERBET $1.50

NEW YORK STYLE CHEESECAKE $2.75
        with blueberry or cherry $3.00

PRODUCER'S HOT FUDGE DELIGHT
Chocolate fudge brownies served with vanilla ice cream and smothered with
hot fudge, whipped cream, nuts and a cherry. $4.25

CARAMEL PECAN BALL
Vanilla ice cream rolled in pecans and served with caramel sauce. . $3.95

CAROUSEL STRAWBERRY YOGURT PIE DELUXE
A health conscious dessert of frozen strawberry yogurt topped with a
reasonably generous serving of whipped cream and garnished with a
strawberry slice. The ideal dessert for your winter diet! $2.75

BAKED CINNAMON APPLE
A true seasonal delight! A whole apple dusted with cinnamon and wrapped
in a flaky pastry and baked. Topped with a light cinnamon sauce and
served with ice cream. $4.25

FEED ME MUD PIE!
This is The PLANT'S favorite! Devilishly delicious layers of crushed oreos and
heath bars, chocolate cream and fudge served in a flower pot complete
with a bloom that you can take home and nurture! $4.25

A charge will be made for coffee/tea once the performance begins.

PRODUCER'S SPECIAL
Entrees

These entrees are the Producer's personal favorites.
(Available at an additional charge.)

LOBSTER TAIL
Cold water lobster tail broiled with lemon and sherry. Served with wild rice and seasonal vegetable. $12.95

FILET MIGNON
Center cut tenderloin prepared to order and topped with Bearnaise Sauce and a mushroom cap. Served with a twice baked potato and seasonal vegetable. (The Producer recommends that you ask to have your filet butterflied if you prefer a medium-well or well preparation.) $6.95

BROILED SEAFOOD PLATTER
The perfect seafood combination of scallops, shrimp and scrod broiled and served with wild rice and seasonal vegetable. $8.95

VEAL OSCAR
Sauteed veal tenderloin topped with a hollandaise sauce, crabmeat and asparagus. Served with a twice baked potato and seasonal vegetable.
. . . $9.25

RACK OF LAMB
Rack of lamb covered with a honey and dijon mustard sauce and baked to perfection. Garnished with chives and served with wild rice and seasonal vegetable. $8.95

CATCH OF THE DAY
Fresh catch delivered daily and prepared to the chef's delight! Ask your server for today's special. $9.95

DIRECTOR'S CUT OF PRIME RIB
Your favorite house entree is now available in a cut that even the Director is excited about. 14 ounces! Prepared to your specifications and served with a twice baked potato and seasonal vegetable. (Due to the popularity of this entree, end-cuts may not always be available.) $5.75

APPETIZERS
Indulge Yourself

Wisconsin Cheddar Ale Soup $2.50
A creamy combination of Wisconsin's finest cheddar and hearty ale.

Baked Mushrooms $3.50
A baked crock topped with provolone and cheddar cheeses.

Baked Brie $4.95
Warmed brie cheese topped with toasted almonds and served with fresh fruit and french bread.

Appetizer Platter $5.95
A generous assortment of our own special meatballs, peel and eat shrimp, and our creamy seafood spread served with crackers.

Cheese Curds $3.95
The dairyland's pride dipped in our own seasoned batter and deep-fried to a golden brown.

DESSERTS
The Perfect Ending

Towards the end of your meal, your server will introduce you to Fanny Hill's fabulous desserts. A bounty of goodies all freshly prepared in our own kitchen. From traditional favorites to the truly unique, there's something to satisfy every sweet tooth.

Fanny Hill Inn & Dinner Theatre. Eau Claire, Wisconsin.

ENTREES

Chicken and Crab Alfredo

Sauteed boneless breast of chicken and tender crabmeat topped with a creamy parmesan sauce and served with linguine.

Seafood Le Creme Supreme

Broiled haddock ladled with scallops and shrimp in a light cream sauce and served on a bed of blended rice.

Oahu Pork

Marinated boneless cutlets of pork grilled and glazed with our pineapple sweet and sour sauce.

Shrimp Bechamel

Jumbo gulf shrimp filled with a crabmeat stuffing and served in a rich cream sauce.

Chicken Bigarade

A boneless breast of chicken filled with wild rice and sausage stuffing and finished with an orange burgundy sauce.

ADDITIONAL COST

Prime Rib $3.95

Slow-cooked to perfection and served aujus.

New York Strip $3.95

Thick boneless cut. The king of steaks.

THE OVERTURE
A delicious beginning to a wonderful meal

APPETIZERS

SHRIMP COCKTAIL $5.95
*Mouth-watering shrimp served with
lemon and tangy cocktail sauce.*

STUFFED MUSHROOM CAPS $4.25
*Filled with the Ascot's famous
cream cheese and herbs.*

FRENCH ONION SOUP $2.95
*Our own recipe! Made from 3 varieties of
sharp, zesty onions, topped with melted
domestic cheeses.*

ICE-COLD SEAFOOD PLATTER
*$6.25 per person
Smoked salmon, crab claws and shrimp
served with marinated vegetables.*

CHEESE AND FRUIT PLATTER FOR 2 OR 4 $2.95 per person
A tempting array of imported and domestic cheeses complimented by the freshest fruits available.

THE CAESAR SALAD $2.95
*Romaine lettuce, vinegar, olive oil, anchovies,
Parmesan cheese and croutons, tossed our own special way.*

THE ASCOT THEATRE MATINEE
TICKET PRICE INCLUDES:

1 entree, Ascot salad (Our Special House Dressing), assorted rolls and butter, coffee or tea

ENTREE

STUFFED FILET OF FLOUNDER
*Delicious Crab meat dressing encased by a
boneless Flounder and finished with a sublime
tarragon sauce. Rice pilaf and the fresh
vegetable of the day make this meal a treat.*

CHICKEN AMBROSIA
*Chicken breast, boneless and skinless, baked
then highlighted with olive oil, lemon, honey
and fresh fruit. Served with rice and the fresh
vegetable of the day.*

LONDON BROIL
*Marinated, broiled and thinly sliced served
with a mushroom sauce and house potato.*

*STEAMED FRESH
VEGETABLE PLATE*
An assortment of fresh seasonal vegetables.

*This item may be prepared according to *HEALTHMARK* guidelines.

Note: Ticket price includes show and dinner. Other beverages, appetizers, desserts and gratuity are not
included. For the purpose of tipping, your meal is valued at $9.00 of the dinner theatre ticket.

Ascot Dinner Theatre. Littleton, Colorado.

SPECIALTY ENTREES

(not included in the regular ticket price)
(please allow a little extra time for preparation and serving)

For Your Special Occasion
Includes the vegetable of the day and your choice of potato or rice pilaf.

BROILED SALMON FILET $6.95
Fresh Pacific salmon, hand-fillet, thickly sliced and broiled, enhanced with a béarnaise sauce.

TOURNEDOS ASCOT $9.95
Tenderloin medallions served with shrimp and artichoke, demi-glace and béarnaise sauce.

AUSTRALIAN ROCK LOBSTER TAIL MARKET PRICE
8 oz. Rock Lobster tail, broiled, accompanied by drawn butter.

For quicker service at intermission, we suggest you pre-order your beverage and dessert prior to the start of the performance.

ENCORE!

DESSERTS

THE SOUND OF MUSIC $3.50
A chocolate cup filled with raspberry melba and Haagen-Dazs ice-cream served with a special chocolate topping.

BANANAS FOSTER $3.50
Sliced bananas flambe' with rum, almonds, brown sugar, cinnamon, citrus juices, over ice cream .

STRAWBERRY SHORTCAKE $2.95
Sweet shortbread with ice cream , fresh strawberries and whipped cream.

BAKED ALASKA $3 per person
(For 2, 4 or 6)
24 hours advance notice, please.

SPECIALTY DESSERT TRAY $3.95 each
Presented by your server

ICE CREAM AND SHERBET $2.25

We serve Coca-Cola *as our exclusive cola beverage.   We proudly feature* Häagen-Dazs *ice cream.*
The Ascot Theatre serves Farmer Brothers Coffee.
We recommend gourmet flavors of the international award-winning The Incredible Cheesecake ®

Chanhassen
Dinner Theatre
Menu

Your ticket includes: our Caesar salad, an entree
selection with appropriate accompaniments, and a
bottomless cup of McGarvey Colombian coffee

USDA CHOICE TOP SIRLOIN STEAK

BREAST OF CHICKEN PARMESAN
Sauteed lightly with Parmesan cheese and herbs

ROAST LOIN of PORK SMITANE
with escalloped apples and a sour
cream and mustard sauce

SEAFOOD TORTELLINI PRIMAVERA
with shrimp and scallops

A La Carte Appetizers

SMOKY CHEDDAR CHEESE SPREAD
with assorted crackers
$3.50

JUMBO SHRIMP COCKTAIL
$6.95

VIETNAMESE STYLE EGG ROLLS
with CHICKEN WINGS
and two sauces
$4.25

BUFFALO CHICKEN WINGS AND
BEER BATTERED CHEESE STICKS
for two $5.95

TODAY'S SOUP
$2.75

A La Carte Entrees

T-BONE STEAK
with Crisp Onion Rings
$4.95

GRILLED FRESH NORWEGIAN SALMON FILLET
$3.95

Please ask about today's special

Chanhassen Dinner Theatre. Chanhassen, Minnesota.

Chanhassen Dinner Theatres

CHAPTER 4

The "Theatre" in Dinner Theatre

THE THEATRES

Dinner theatres vary widely in the type of stage used and the format of productions presented. Depending on the size and physical layout of a facility, arena stages (in-the-round), proscenium stages, proscenium thrust stages, and three-quarter stages are all utilized. Both complex, elaborate multi-faceted sets and simple, compact set pieces can be used in virtually all theatre types depending on the show, artistic discretion, and the budget. A producer may spend anywhere from $500 to $100,000 for set construction for a single dinner theatre production.

According to Marc Resnik, associate producer for the Carousel Dinner Theatre in Akron: "Both scenery and costumes in today's dinner theatres must be more intricate and exciting than those of 15 or 20 years ago. The audiences of today are much more visually oriented—based largely on their conditioning through special effects in movies and on television. Because they're expecting to see 'spectacles' on stage, the 1950s *Honeymooners* interior set just won't do." He feels that the overall adult attention span has decreased and that people need to see more variety in a shorter time span. Whether an arena-type stage or a large proscenium is used, the visual aspects of sets and costumes must be appealing.

THE SHOWS

The types of productions that seem to be most widely accepted in dinner theatre are referred to as the "old war-horses." These are musical productions with tunes that audiences can hum as they leave. Most were highly successful on Broadway, and patrons are familiar with at least the titles, if not the story lines. Some of these musicals include *Singin' in the Rain*; *The Boy Friend*; *Damn Yankees*; *Anything Goes*; *Can-Can*; *Brigadoon*; *Camelot*; *Carousel*; *Fiddler on the Roof*, *42nd Street*; *Guys and Dolls*; *Hello, Dolly!*; *Mame*; *I Do, I Do!*; *The King and I*; *The Music Man*; *The Sound of Music*; *South Pacific*; *West Side Story*; *Man of La Mancha*; *Grease*; *Evita*; *Annie*; *Ain't Misbehavin'*; *A Chorus Line*; *Cabaret*; *The Fantasticks*; *Sugar Babies*; *Nunsense*; and *Oklahoma!*.

Straight plays, which include popular comedies and new works, are also produced in dinner theatres, especially in a multi-theatre operation, such as the Dinner Playhouses in Kansas City or the Chanhassen in Minnesota, although most dinner theatres are sticking to musical productions. When a straight play is produced, it's likely to be a tried-and-true favorite, such as *Social Security*; *Barefoot in the Park*; *The Last of the Red Hot Lovers*; *Murder at the Howard Johnson's*; *The Sunshine Boys*; *Same Time, Next Year*; *Play It Again, Sam*; *Biloxi Blues*; *Brighton Beach Memoirs*; *God's Favorite*; or *Everybody Loves Opal*. Neil Simon's plays are wonderful for the dinner theatre circuit because they involve small casts, are easy to produce, can be star vehicles, and are box office draws.

The running length of musicals or straight plays can be as short as four weeks and up to twenty-seven weeks, but the average run is about eight weeks. The length will also depend on whether or not the theatre has a season-subscription program. *I Do, I Do!* has been running on one of the three stages at the Chanhassen Dinner Theatre for 20 years.

TECHNICAL ASPECTS

It would be tremendous if one chapter of this book could be devoted to the technical aspects of theatrical productions in all dinner theatres, but that would be next to impossible because all dinner theatres are different. Factors that vary include the vast scheduling differences between theatres, the varying stage and scenery formats, differences in production values, and availability of on-hand materials as opposed to rented, purchased, or in-house-created materials.

Some dinner theatres close a production and set up for another show in 24 hours, as in the case of a celebrity attraction that runs between musicals. Several days later, a new long-running musical may open with only one dark day. Some theatres may be dark for several weeks between productions. In that case, their set-construction parameters would be different than if a theatre had only a few days to put up a show.

Some dinner theatres use the arena style, also known as in-the-round. The sets for this stage format must be constructed so that they can be seen from all areas of the theatre; and individual pieces must be lightweight and easily movable. A proscenium theatre can make much larger and more elaborate sets that can be flown in from above or rolled in, and they needn't be seen from the back side, for example.

Very small dinner theatres, which seat, for example, only 90 would probably have a relatively smaller budget than a theatre seating 1,200. Aside from the cost factor, size and sometimes quality differences exist.

Finally, each production may vary according to internal factors, such as the materials that are already in the theatre, as opposed to what needs to be constructed, purchased, rented, or borrowed. These include costumes, props, sets, sound and lighting equipment, and special-effects equipment.

It is apparent that technical facilities are seldom the same among dinner theatres. Each operation begins with its budget, and the remaining considerations are adapted to its facility and its capabilities. Dinner theatres do share sets, props, and costumes but, with few exceptions, it is rare that a show will be transferred in its entirety from one dinner theatre to another.

Auditions

Each week, *Back Stage*, the performing arts weekly published in New York City, contains numerous dinner theatre audition options for both union and non-union actors residing in New York and across the country. The union dinner theatres have auditions in New York, Los Angeles, Chicago, and other major metropolitan areas. Non-union theatres hold local auditions and often join together for regional auditions, once each year, with the NDTA (National Dinner Theatre Association) and the SETC (Southeastern Theatre Conference). At auditions an actor must be prepared to demonstrate singing, dancing, and acting abilities; these auditions are like other acting auditions held throughout the country. The union dinner theatres across the country must subscribe to fairness in the audition and hiring process and support equal opportunity rights for all actors, as stated in the national contract.

THE ACTUAL EXPERIENCE FOR THE ACTOR

Often, an actor who has never worked in a dinner theatre will wonder what the experience would be like. An actor we will call Alan will be our example here. He is a union actor and has been hired by a union producer at a medium-size-to-large dinner theatre. After holding auditions in New York, the producer contacts Alan to offer him a chorus contract for the musical *Oliver!*. He explains the parts Alan will be playing. Alan's base salary will be $412.25 per week. Since he will be hired also as the assistant stage manager for the musical, he'll receive an additional $41.50 per week. Alan will also be playing one extra chorus role at $16.00 extra per week and one principal role (Mr. Sowerberry) at $32.00 more per week. He will understudy one role at no additional compensation and another role at an additional $20.00 per week. Because Alan will be using his own shoes ($2.50) in the musical and his own overcoat ($5.00) perfect for the role, he'll receive an extra $7.50 per week. Alan's total weekly income is $529.25.

Alan accepts the job and the contract is mailed to him. The producer makes Alan's travel arrangements and sends him airline tickets. Alan will be paid to get from his apartment in New York City to La Guardia Airport. He will be picked up at the local airport near the theatre and transported to the theatre or to the cast apartment house. Several weeks later, Alan in fact arrives and is taken to the cast apartments. He is placed in a two-bedroom apartment and is sharing with an actor we will call Peter. Rent is $75 per week for each actor. Transportation to and from the theatre is provided. Alan begins a paid 10-day rehearsal period to prepare for the show. Alan is taken, during a split rehearsal period, to be fitted for the costumes he'll be wearing. The rehearsals are staggered from 10:00 a.m. to 10:00 p.m. during the first week. However, Alan rehearses only seven hours out of a possible eight and one-half hours.

The show opens on a Wednesday night and the director's notes are given afterward. The theatre opens to patrons at 6:00 p.m., dinner service starts at 6:15, and the curtain goes up at 8:30. The show is over at 10:55. The Thursday-night call is for 8:00. Evening shows are on Tuesday, Wednesday, Thursday, Friday, Saturday, and Sunday. Matinees are on Wednesday and Saturday and the day off is Monday. The run of the show is eight weeks.

Alan and the other cast members often spend their free time during the day sleeping in, running errands, working out, shopping, or socializing. On a Friday afternoon there will be a brush-up rehearsal and on the next Friday there will be a brush-up dance rehearsal at 12:00 noon. On the following Monday night the cast will have a "progressive dinner," going to each of their apartments in the complex.

During the sixth week the producer posts a closing notice, to remind the actors that the show will indeed be closing in two weeks, and that scripts and company property must be returned so that their final paychecks can then be given out. Return transportation arrangements are made by the producer. Sunday night's show is the closing performance and Alan is on his way to the airport Monday afternoon.

PROBLEMS WITH PERFORMERS

Not only do theatre owners and operators have to work closely with the public, their staff, vendors, and other related business people, but they must also deal fairly with problems that arise with performers.

Owners, operators, and producers have indicated the existence of some common problems—ongoing issues that are related to talent. Most of the actors working in dinner theatre today are elated just to be working. But there seems also to be a growing trend in many theatres where problems are arising much more often, although owners are aware that problems are present in every profession and that theirs is no different.

Love of Craft?

In the performing arts, people study for years to perfect their discipline. Time, pain, and effort are often expended for the sake of their "love of the craft." And then, as is the goal of others, the performer hopes to become a professional, to be paid for what he or she loves to do.

Unfortunately, not all actors achieve the wealth, success, or status that they may seek. The lucky breaks don't occur for everyone and moonlighting can become the actor's permanent mainstay. Yet, there are those who, through talent, perseverance, and some luck, work regularly in the performing arts—more specifically, on the dinner theatre circuit. But in this group of working actors, there are those who take for granted the employment that they have studied and waited for. Some take advantage of the producers, their fellow actors, and the art form to which they have become committed.

Work Ethics

Because of these "problem actors," some producers ask: "What happened to the time when an actor took great pride in the work he did and the theatre he worked for; when he would go the extra mile for his employer and for the good of the company and of his fellow actors; when he would follow the rules and be a team player?" In fact, pride among actors is still alive. Even though it may not be as prevalent as it was 50 years ago, it still exists.

Among a newer generation of actors, there seems to be an increasing group of performers who cast a negative light on those fellow actors who believe in what they do and present themselves in a professional manner. The concerns of these newer, younger actors (and of some seasoned performers) relate mainly to themselves. Their egos, along with their apathy, create an attitude toward work-related problems that says: "It's the producer's problem," or "Let the union worry about it."

The idea of "one for all and all for one" may be slowly vanishing from the theatre work place, for a variety of reasons. This absence of group spirit can directly influence an entire cast and the quality of a production. The adage "The show must go on!" may indeed be reminiscent of a bygone era.

Considering that the majority of actors are a tribute to the acting profession—dedicated and talented—the following accounts given by dinner theatre producers can be eye openers. As one producer said: "We have to take the bad with the good."

Who's Being Represented?

One gripe from producers has surfaced repeatedly. Certain agents, supposedly representing actors, are preventing these actors from accepting work because the agents are holding out for what they may consider to be a better job just around the corner. Certainly a higher-paying job for an actor is preferred (and so is a higher agent's commission); however, if the job never materializes, the actor is the person who suffers the most. The actor may never have known about the producer's offer. Also, the actor should be aware that some agents have been trying to tell producers how to run their businesses. Several producers will no longer deal with certain agents because of this attitude. In all cases these are not very ethical treatments in the representation of actors.

Getting Paid for What They Don't Do

One of the saddest of comments came from an actor who was offered a contract that didn't meet his approval. His response to the producer was, "No, thanks. I'd be better off on unemployment." It should also be noted here that a producer, somewhere, is paying into a fund so that actors can have unemployment benefits if the situation should arise; it's the law. It appears that the producers do need a mechanism for informing the various employment boards that an offer has been made and turned down by the performer or by the performer's agent.

Pets and Weddings in the Act

As unbelievable as it may seem, professionals are turning down employment if their pets (dogs, cats, lizards) cannot come with them. Those with clout will insist that such a demand be negotiated into their contract. Will family, friends, and their high-school graduating class be next?

One young actress was dismayed to discover that during the run of the production in which she was to appear, she would be missing a family wedding. In a field where the unemployment rate is relatively high, it is astonishing to see that employment contracts are hinging on fringe benefits such as days off, pets, and accommodations. Incidentally, the producer did give her the time off for the wedding.

Free Housing but at a Price

The word "free" has a distorted meaning in today's advertising. There is very little (if anything) that is actually free; one will pay, in some form or another, for whatever is received. Most housing for cast members is expensive for any producer. If a producer should opt not to charge for housing that is provided (which is rare), then this "complimentary" housing is paid for by the performers in the form of lower salaries. It certainly can be of great benefit to the performers, but in actuality it isn't free to the producer or to the performers.

Inconsiderate Producer Gives Day Off

Virtually the entire cast of a dinner theatre production was reportedly up in arms because a producer decided to give the cast an extra day off—with pay! Ticket sales were low for the next day's performance, so the producer made a judgment call, cancelled the performance, and gave the cast the day off with pay. Shortly after the announcement, a cast member called the producer to express his anger. He felt the producer was very rude and inconsiderate to cancel without due notice to the cast. He explained that members of the cast were unable to participate in auditions that they could have attended, had they been given more notice. With restraint, the producer explained that he could have required the actors to perform before an empty house, or just have made them sit in the theatre for three hours. He chose to let them have the day off with pay. Imagine what the cast might have done if he had given them two days off.

Commitments—Hard to Spell Out, Hard to Keep

It was reported that one star performer confirmed that he would keep a television engagement to promote a dinner theatre's show. Fifteen minutes prior to the airing, while the network affiliate involved was setting up in the theatre for the live remote broadcast, the performer decided not to do the broadcast. Why? He had no reason other than, "I'm not going to do it." This put the producer and the television station in an awkward situation, to say the least. Arrogance, irresponsibility, and lack of professionalism have marred this performer's reputation. This type of attitude even seemed to pervade the ranks of the newest actors in the company.

Dealing with No-shows

No producer will deny an actor the opportunity to work as often as possible—unless the additional work is during their contracted time and with another producer. One East Coast producer constantly faces the problem of contracted actors who miss rehearsals, half-hour calls, and performances to audition for television commercials, soaps and industrials. The problem, the producer says, is that one has to prove that actors do this. It's common knowledge why the actors are missing (and calling in sick), but the producer must have the hard evidence in order to bring the matter up for disciplinary action.

This type of situation confronted another producer. An actor claimed that he could not finish the run of a musical because of illness. He was found performing shortly thereafter on a cruise ship. Even though the actor allegedly violated his contract and misrepresented his situation so that he could obtain additional work, the producer would have to spend considerable money and time to prove the facts. Must producers be detectives, attorneys, and babysitters in order to run their theatres effectively?

IS TRUE ENSEMBLE WORK GONE?

Perhaps there is too much emphasis now being placed on the quality of workmanship. Or, is the theatre work force gradually mutating into a group of disassociated performers who clock in and out, and is true ensemble work becoming a thing of the past? If so, who is to blame?

For a possible answer, one might look to the fast-paced, mass-production-type society that surrounds the theatrical world. Some believe that today's generation may be prone to lower work standards and more inclined to focus on egocentricity and self-promotion at any cost. An "honest dollar earned for a hard day's work" seems to be a valid concept for fewer individuals today. This dilemma may supersede the problems that producers are facing at their theatres and may be pervading society as a whole.

Again, there are many quality performers, and there will always be the "squeaky wheels" who get the oil. Producers would like to believe the latter are in the minority and do not reflect the thousands of actors who are top-notch professionals, whether seasoned actors or budding young performers.

It is apparent that exceptional theatre exists throughout the country and it will continue to thrive, in spite of those who differ in thinking and ethics from the rest. Their actions make it more difficult for producers of dinner theatre to provide the quality theatre that people have grown accustomed to and certainly deserve.

ACTORS' PROFILES

It's always a pleasure to profile the careers of performers who have "paid their dues." Though their names may not be familiar to the general public, Jacquiline Rohrbacker and David Brummel have worked in almost all areas of live theatre—including regional theatre, Broadway, and dinner theatre. In the profiles below, Rohrbacker and Brummel discuss their careers and their opinions about the theatre world. By looking at the path that each has taken, one can better understand how they have achieved the level of success they both are enjoying, and perhaps what it takes to get there.

SHE BEGAN AS A SINGER

Jacquiline Rohrbacker often returns to her home in Fort Collins, Colorado, when she's not working on a particular role. Jacquiline is best known for the many character roles she has played over the past 24 years.

She obtained a Bachelor of Arts degree in instrumental music from Colorado State University, intending to teach music. While taking two semesters of voice, a vocal teacher insisted that she audition for the Central City Opera Company in Colorado. Two weeks later, she received a chorus contract in the mail. Jacquiline performed during the summer season at Central City and then began a two-year job teaching junior high school. A friend recommended that she audition for the Santa Fe Opera. Again, she was selected and she sang with the company for one season. This led to another position, with the Dallas Opera Company, and then to another, with a theatre-in-the-round in Fort Worth. At this theatre, Casa Mañana,

Jacquiline first discovered her real joy—musical comedy—as she had a chance to play a small role and also to be in the chorus. She loved it. After two seasons, her vocal coach explained to Jacquiline that she was ready for New York and to take the chance. She did.

A Move to the Big Apple

To help support herself, Jacquiline was hired as a sales clerk at Lord & Taylor. She was also lucky enough to have a steady church job as a vocal soloist. She auditioned for the Metropolitan Opera Company. They asked her to sing and dance. She was hired to fill in for someone who had left the company abruptly; the singer had not only performed various roles, but was also featured in one of the dance numbers. She feels that because she had a little tap experience, it helped her get the job.

She went on tour for one and one-half seasons, and it seemed that doors were now opening for her. What did she do to allow this to happen? Jacquiline feels that she always gave her best effort at her performances, regardless of the size of the role she played. "You never know who will be watching you—either cast, crew, or the audience. Always perform at 100 percent of your ability," exclaimed Rohrbacker.

This philosophy worked for her when she was performing with the John Kenley Company in Ohio. During a show, Kenley was in the audience, unbeknownst to Jacquiline, watching her to determine if she would be suitable for another role—a lead role in *Annie Get Your Gun.* She would play Dolly Tate, opposite Florence Henderson. Jacquiline recalled, "Florence had final casting approval and watched my performance with John. She and John approved and I got the part."

Not only did she act, sing, and dance with Kenley, but she also learned all the aspects of the theatre from him. She said: "Years later, I asked John if I could work behind the scenes to learn more about the business. I worked in the box office, as a dresser, as a costumer, as a company spokesperson, as an ASM [assistant stage manager], and in advertising sales. I now have a deep respect for all of the hard work done by everyone else, because I did it, too. I always kept an open mind to all areas of the profession since you never know what small changes can lead you to."

It was the national tour of *George M!* that really let Rohrbacker shine in the musical comedy medium. Since then she has appeared with various symphony orchestras doing pop concerts and Christmas cantatas; however, her emphasis has turned toward playing character roles, adding her own zany twist to them. It appears that Rohrbacker had lady luck on her side, especially during the earlier years of her career. Each audition seemed to result in a job. Even though Rohrbacker admits to having had some luck, she says that rejection can really hurt. She still gets nervous at auditions but she keeps on telling herself, "Just do your best."

Rejection Hits Hard

She notes: "While I was doing opera, I had been given a lead role that was in my contract. I began rehearsing the part and worked very hard on it. A friend in the company told me to check the board because someone else was evidently put into the role and rehearsing it behind my back. No one told me a thing. I later found out, by talking to the director, that I had been replaced because they felt I didn't have the experience at that point to handle a large role."

Did she accept that explanation or was she hurt? "I cried for days," she says. "As a matter of fact, I sat in my car and cried so that I wouldn't have to let the company see me in tears." Seven years later, history repeated itself, although she was now on the other side of the fence. The same situation occurred with someone else and Jacquiline was asked to step in for her. Remembering the trauma that she had felt, Rohrbacker insisted that the girl have everything explained to her before she (Rohrbacker) would step onto the rehearsal stage. And it was duly explained.

Not all of her auditions got her jobs, but all of her auditions were successes, Rohrbacker says, in that she learned from every audition; and from every show she was in. "And I did make mistakes. I didn't really know how to work properly with an agent. I'd leave town and not tell my agent that I was away. Things would come up and I'd miss an opportunity. Another big mistake was that I auditioned for shows that I was totally wrong for. Even though I learned from it, it was a waste of valuable time. It became very depressing."

Words of Advice

For the new actors now getting into the business, Rohrbacker also advocates "keeping in touch" with people. She said that she auditioned for a particular job, but didn't get it. She remained positive. In a hallway after the audition, she spoke with an individual who said, "Where have you been?" And by talking, she got another job through that person. She noted: "You never know who can help you. When people say, 'Contact me,' that's exactly what they mean. And you should. They're not just saying that to be nice.

"There are two fields worse than acting for competition: politics and sports. To get the edge, come to auditions prepared and follow up with phone calls and mailings. It takes self-discipline."

Comparing today's talent scene with that of two decades ago, Rohrbacker feels that there are fewer opportunities today: "The quality talent is certainly there—there's so much more, but there seem to be fewer jobs now. Back then, if you couldn't get a job during the year, there were always summer stock jobs available. It's different now. Directors are taking less chances with newer actors.

"Another thing that's different is that an actor could get hired then much more easily if he or she only sang, danced, or read. Today you have to be a 'triple threat.' Because of the type of shows today, like *Phantom* and *Les Miserables*, you need to give a very strong performance in at least two of the three areas."

An Established Performer

Rohrbacker feels comfortable with what she does in the business. She has been fortunate to perform major roles alongside such stars as Shirley Jones, Florence Henderson, Sonny Bono, Carol Lawrence, Tommy Tune, Joe Namath, the late Gordon MacRae, and Vincent Price. Between 1982 and 1989, she performed on the S.S. *Norway* in *My Fair Lady* and *42nd Street*. "It's one of the ships that has the facility for a full-scale Broadway-level show," she says. She enjoys her character work in dinner theatres all over the country: "I love doing dinner theatre because there's a closeness with the cast, crew, and with the audience. I feel that I want to say to them, 'Relax, drink, eat, and have fun!' It's like a grand [get-together]: 'Let's sit in the living room, get comfortable, and watch the show.' "

What's next for Jacquiline Rohrbacker? "Well, you know, I tell students that I lecture that they must take chances. I'm fairly well settled with what I'm doing, but one of my goals is that I want to pursue comedy sitcoms in Los Angeles. It would be a new adventure for me. I know I'd have to move out there, and it would be a big change for me, but, I've got to take the chance. Everyone has their insecurities in different ways. But, if you do care about your work and what you do, you will be nervous. Take chances. You never know what will come up in the future. Maintain your self-confidence. Believe in yourself!"

A CHANGE IN HIS CAREER

David Brummel owned a furniture store in New London, Connecticut. A friend asked him to audition for a play at a community theatre in the

area. He did, and got a role in the comedy, *A Thousand Clowns*. During
the run, another local director was interested in possibly using David in
Bye Bye Birdie. He knew of David's singing talent through a church choir
he was in. David auditioned and was cast.

Something inside David said, "It's time to change." At age 28 he made
the decision to sell his furniture business and move to New York.

On the Monday morning he arrived in New York, Brummel bought a
copy of *Variety* to look for current stage auditions (he knew of no other
trade publication). He read a notice for a Don and Gina King Showcase
for Singers on the East Side, held at a club called Pal Joey's every Monday
night. He sang there. A performer that evening was reading a copy of *Back
Stage* and it made David curious. "What is that?" he questioned. The
performer explained and Brummel got a copy of *Back Stage* from a
newsstand. He noticed that a dinner theatre in New Jersey needed a lyric
baritone for a musical. On Wednesday he went there, read, sang, and was
cast in a lead role at the Club Bene. Appearing with Meg Bussart, Jimmy
Brennan, and a 17-year-old John Travolta in the chorus, Brummel's New
York career began. He was paid $65 per week, which included one meal
and transportation. This show ran four weeks and David continued there
in the next show. Afterward, Brummel's road travels began as a director
cast him in a production of *Man of La Mancha* in Pittsburgh.

His Stepping Stone

His experience as a part of the Lakewood Musical Theatre is what
Brummel considers to be his most valuable asset—a stepping stone during
that time. This non-Equity summer stock in Pennsylvania produced 11
musicals in 12 weeks. Brummel recounts, "I learned the most I ever did
here [at Lakewood], especially the technique of learning quickly. It also
provided a great instant résumé."

Other avenues were now accessible to him as well. He performed in the
national tour of *Man of La Mancha*; in the Los Angeles company of *Evita*;
in *42nd Street*; *Nine*; and *Zorba*, with Anthony Quinn. He was also part
of the record-breaking Japanese tour of *West Side Story*. On Broadway he
performed in a revival of *The Pajama Game*; in *Music Is, Annie, Nine,
Evita*, and *Oklahoma!*. Later, he was cast in various films, such as *A
Stranger Is Watching, Bums, Dog Day Afternoon*, and *Taxi Driver*. His
soap-opera work includes "All My Children" and "Search for Tomorrow."
He has worked opposite such stars as Betsy Palmer, in *South Pacific*;
Barbara Eden, in *Annie Get Your Gun*; Karen Mason, in *Funny Girl*; Dixie
Carter, in *Kiss Me Kate*; and Cloris Leachman, in *Wonderful Town*.

Thinking Back

Does David have any regrets or are there mistakes that he made during his career? He replies: "I seldom said no to a job. I've spent a tremendous amount of time on the road. Where the mistake comes in is that many times I've lost out on jobs that were happening in New York. I do love this business and what I do. And, I treat it as a business. I love to work and won't just sit around. I've been on the road for a total of about 15 or 16 years! Sometimes I regret some of those missed opportunities."

Starting Out Today

For actors starting out today, Brummel gives this advice: "Get as much experience as you can, especially in non-Equity operations. There you can do a variety of shows and variations of parts. Do that for several years. Don't be hell-bent on immediately joining SAG or Equity. If you do luck into an Equity show at the beginning, remember that you're up against the best. Hold off on getting that [Equity] card for a while. Equity operations are going to cast for only the very best for any role. Get that experience first, both professionally and emotionally."

Succeeding in the acting business involves a combination of a number of factors. Brummel emphasizes: "Do your job. Get along with everyone. Learn, listen, and watch. Watch the good actors as well as the bad ones. [People] can survive in this business if their abilities are average—as long as they can get along well with others and be valuable company members. Those who get hired over and over again are the actors without an attitude. Be grateful you're doing what you love doing."

Theatre Trends

Brummel cites several trends: "English theatre has changed things here. Twenty years ago there may have been 25-to-30 shows up and down Broadway. Today there may be 10. Economics are different now. Actors, too, must be more versatile. When I did *Pajama Game* on Broadway, there were eight female dancers, eight male dancers, eight female singers, and eight male singers. Companies are now half as large, with cast members doing combinations of things." He advises: "Because there is more competition, learn to do as much as you possibly can. You've got to be able to do much more today to beat the competition.

"I can't even tell you how many actors I started with 21 years ago who are no longer in the business. Longevity is an issue. Not only does it take talent, but it takes marketing. Be aware of what your own 'type' is—your product. You are also a salesman who sells. Package and sell yourself correctly."

This same thinking applies to the auditioning process. Brummel says: "Learn what you are—[how] other people see you; [how] a director may see you. I kept auditioning for a director for seven or eight years and would not get cast. It got to the point that I thought he hated me. Finally he did cast me. I asked him afterward if he disliked me. The director said 'not at all.' " The director said further that he felt David had great talent, but the "chemistry" for the particular roles he sought was just not right. Then finally it was.

Brummel says: "If you ever get a callback, consider yourself good enough to do the role. At that point it's not talent, it's chemistry."

Doing Movies?

David Brummel classifies himself as a leading character man. He was told in the past that he was too young looking for leading roles in films. Now he's thinking more about this medium. He said: "The last eight years have been really important for me, doing all the nationals and leading roles. Now I think I'd like to do a little more with films since I'm not quite as young looking now." When asked what his goal is, Brummel chuckled, "I want to continue to work."

BOTH HAD LUCK, A POSITIVE ATTITUDE

What Rohrbacker and Brummel have admitted is that they were both lucky in the advancement of their careers. Neither had many side jobs unrelated to performing. Both basically got what they auditioned for. Doors opened for them and their careers sprouted.

Both actors discussed mistakes and disappointments that happen to all performers during their careers. It's how they handled them that seems to make the difference. A positive attitude and common sense can go a long way.

They both also expressed the need for the competitive edge—the versatility and marketing savvy that are so important for newer actors. Packaging and marketing, along with talent and perseverance, may very well be the keys to success in the competitive performing medium.

DINNER THEATRE STARS

Where do the young actors go today to get their start in professional acting? They go to dinner theatres. For over 30 years, budding young actors have often gotten their initial acting experiences on dinner theatre stages across the country. And for some, stardom became a reality.

Because dinner theatre has developed a reputation for offering tremendous value, there are, unfortunately, some individuals who still view dinner theatres as "second rate" entertainment facilities, beneath legitimate houses. To the contrary, many of the Equity-affiliated dinner theatres are well-managed, high-quality theatres that are second to none. These dinner theatres have been, and continue to be, a top-notch proving ground for countless numbers of talented actors and are also a venue for returning stars of every magnitude.

Tony D'Angelo, co-producer of Chicago's Candlelight Dinner Playhouse, America's First Dinner Theatre, feels that dinner theatre has much to offer for new talent: "We help each other. They go out and develop their skills and then return. They're grateful they had the chance." D'Angelo discussed many of the actors who started at the Candlelight and later went on to do movies, television, or Broadway. He said, "Mandy Patinkin did his first professional performance with us. He's originally from Chicago and drops in occasionally when he's in town."

The national tour of *Dreamgirls* was mounted at the Candlelight and began its tour schedule there. D'Angelo explained that dinner theatre also provides an excellent medium for local audiences to experience what they might not see unless they go to New York. He said that "when I was younger, summer stock seemed to be everywhere. It was the place for new actors to learn their art through the chorus as well as playing lead roles. Today, it's dinner theatre that serves as a training ground for actors, similar to what Vaudeville was in the past. Here in Chicago, many of our actors will supplement their income by doing television, movies, and children's theatre." But many of these newly groomed actors still aspire to reach Broadway.

Scott Griffith, executive producer/owner of Ohio's Carousel Dinner Theatre, the largest U.S. dinner theatre, is proud of the fact that over 35 performers who had worked at the Carousel (some repeatedly) were later on Broadway at the same time. Marc Resnik, Carousel's associate producer, explained that "we may give many actors their start, but many do give back to us." Susan Cella performed as Evita Peron in *Evita* on Broadway and subsequently returned to the Carousel and starred in their production of *Evita*. Resnik stated that the same was true of David

Brummel, who played Juan Peron in the first national tour and came back to the Carousel to play that same role. Some performers have also gone on to do movie roles and television. Scott Bakula, star of television's "Quantum Leap," performed at the Carousel, filling in as a replacement for an actor who left to do a national tour.

Robert Turoff's Golden Apple Dinner Theatres in Sarasota and Venice, Florida, are further examples of dinner theatres that support the idea of working with and developing quality talent. Bob's wife, Roberta, commented: "We have a large talent pool of actors on the west coast of Florida who stay here year-round." She added that it's like a mini-Chicago. She recalled giving Betty Buckley her Equity card. She said, "Ian Sullivan had starred in one of our shows after returning from New York, where he was in *Shadowlands*." When asked about the importance of guiding fresh, new talent, Roberta replied: "We make our own stars."

Connecticut's Broadway Theatre in Darien also has lists of their actors who have performed on Broadway, toured nationally, done television, done movies, and been nominated for Tony Awards. Jane Bergere, executive producer, states that these individuals include Christopher Hewitt ("Mr. Bellvedere"), Scott Bakula ("Quantum Leap"); Michael Maguire and Jane Lanier (Tony Award nominees); Mark Jacoby, Beth McVey, and Hugh Panaro (*Phantom*); Merwin Foard and Ruth Ann Bigley (*Les Miserables*); and Kristi Carnahan (*Cats*).

Away from Broadway, many dinner theatre performers are now part of national and international tours. Past performers at Chicago's Marriott's Lincolnshire Theatre are travelling through the United States, Canada, and Europe, in such shows as *Aspects of Love*, *Les Miserables*, *Cats*, *A Chorus Line*, and *Phantom of the Opera*.

Dinner theatres not only provide a training ground for talented actors or a "return home" for more accomplished performers, but can also allow actors (and audiences) the ability to experience new theatre. Jan McArt, owner of the Royal Palm Dinner Theatre in Boca Raton, Florida, was the first to produce *The Prince of Central Park*. McArt, according the Bob Bogdanoff, the Royal Palm's artistic director, had met and become friends with Evan Rhodes, who wrote the book for the show. She first agreed to produce the show at her Key West theatre. McArt then moved the production to the Hirschfeld Dinner Theatre in Miami. Afterward it travelled directly to New York, where it premiered on Broadway.

The Showboat Dinner Theatre in Clearwater, Florida, successfully produced a world premiere of a musical, *Denning*, that was selected from the National Alliance of Musical Theatre Producers' two-day Festival of New Musicals. Virginia Sherwood, the Showboat's owner, along with 70 other producers from across the country, is dedicated to bringing to fruition new works for musical theatre. Other dinner theatres involved in this organization are Westchester Broadway Theatre, Marriott's Lincolnshire Theatre, the Royal Palm Dinner Theatre, the Drury Lane Oakbrook Theatre, and the Candlelight Dinner Playhouse. The Alliance has worked with Tony D'Angelo and Bill Pullinsi at the Candlelight to create a version of *Phantom* that can be staged in an arena-style theatre. Obviously, the more new products there are, the more options theatregoers will have. This will also provide more opportunities for all professional actors. Again, dinner theatre is providing more for actors than just a steady source of income.

As already noted, dinner theatre has always been a prime source of training for young, talented actors, and especially now, with the apparent decline of summer stock. The notion that dinner theatre is only a side step for actors, until better opportunities come along, is incorrect, as actors are happily returning to the dinner theatre scene, even after playing leading roles on Broadway. Actors who have made it in television and movies are also grateful that they were able to get the opportunities they did in dinner theatre. With the lack of new products in the theatre world, dinner theatre is certainly doing its part to support musical theatre. Dinner theatres have Actors' Equity's fifth largest national contract for actors in terms of number of work weeks per year; thus the importance and place of dinner theatres within the industry can clearly be seen.

A Chorus Line. Candlelight Dinner Playhouse. Summit, Illinois.

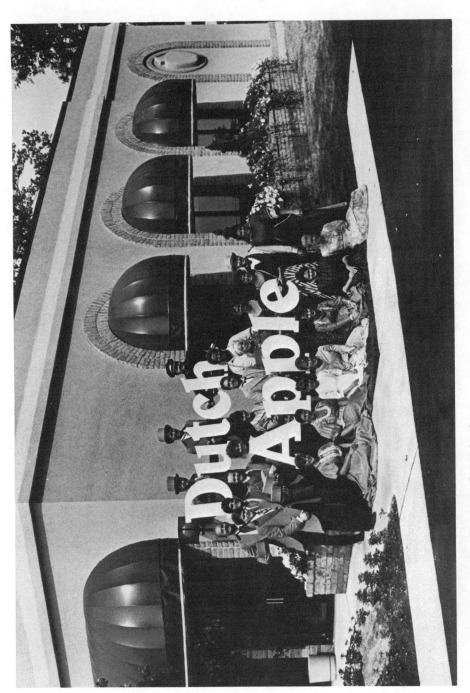

Dutch Apple Dinner Theatre. Lancaster, Pennsylvania.

Set for *The Gazebo*. Garbeau's Dinner Theatre. Rancho Cordova, California.

Candlelight Pavilion. Claremont, California.

42nd Street. Carousel Dinner Theatre. Akron, Ohio.

Carousel Dinner Theatre. Akron, Ohio.

CHAPTER 5

Business Considerations

FINANCIAL PLANNING

Many factors are vital in running a successful dinner theatre. Good financial planning and management is a major consideration for anyone maintaining an existing operation, considering a new location, or contemplating starting a new dinner theatre.

Most people who do not work directly with cost figures are astounded at the enormous expense involved in operating a dinner theatre. Some of those figures were cited by dinner theatre owners and are contained herein. From paying actors to buying beef, sound financial management is essential for any dinner theatre to successfully exist in today's competitive entertainment field.

CONSTRUCTION AND START-UP COSTS

Now that dinner theatre is being marketed more as a business, owners and operators have decided, or, in many instances, have been forced, to either enlarge their operations, modernize, or use other, more suitable facilities. Some have been fortunate enough to plan the construction of a facility or to redesign an existing structure to meet their needs. And yet others are making the bold move of beginning an operation, literally from the ground up. There are certain areas that need to be considered when starting from the beginning.

Four areas are major concerns for the operator who is thinking about moving to a new facility: construction costs, interior-finish expenses, equipment costs, and operating capital. Based on current trends, it can be assumed that a dinner theatre being built today will be approximately 35,000 square feet, will seat 600–700 patrons, and accommodate table service dining. The building may cost between $1.5 million and $2.0 million, depending on frills and site development. If finishing an unused shell, perhaps $1.0–1.2 million should be budgeted. One may add 10 percent for demolition if one is changing an existing finish. Keep in mind that certain site locations (that is, areas of the country) may add considerable cost to construction.

Plan on $700,000 to fully equip the operation. Equipment includes all kitchen hardware: tables, chairs, dishes, glassware, cash registers, and bar equipment. Also, office items, such as furniture, computer hardware/software, copiers, and a security system, must be included. Finally, theatre equipment, such as lighting controls, a lighting system, lamps, a sound system, fire curtains, wardrobe equipment, and stage equipment, need to be considered.

In order to keep a new facility afloat during the pre-operation period, at least $400,000 should be set aside to begin the operation. This money will cover salaries, taxes, advertising, insurance, professional fees, kitchen stocking, telephone costs, other utilities, and first-show pre-production expenses.

Even the best of planners cannot expect the unexpected. Because of possible time delays or miscalculations, a contingency fund, covering all miscellaneous expenses, should be at least $300,000.

The breakdown is as follows (is a leasehold situation is the case):

Interior finish	$1,100,000
Equipment	700,000
Operating capital	400,000
Contingency fund	300,000
TOTAL	$2,500,000

There are several other major considerations to take into account. If a substantial amount of money comes from external financing (that is, 50 percent or $1 million plus), then the cost of obtaining these funds (legal, accounting, and loan) for the pre-operating period could easily run in excess of $100,000. Depending on the rental circumstances, allow for as much as $50,000 in advance lease costs. If the new operation is replacing an existing profitable location and is bringing with it the old audience, a break-even operation could be anticipated from day one. For a new operation, additional capital should be allocated to cover shortfalls for the first 12-18 months of operation.

These figures were recommended by Mark Turpin, executive producer for the Ascot Dinner Theatre in Denver. His operation began in the spring of 1990, from the ground up. Turpin commented on marketing strategy: "Market one year in advance of opening for group business and four months ahead for the general public." Turpin also explained that he made a decision not to utilize the star system. This, he stated, would have increased his yearly costs by between $300,000 and $400,000. With Turpin having done it the right way, critics and audiences have reacted positively to both the food and productions at the newly built Ascot Dinner Theatre.

MOVING THE BUSINESS

One of the dangers for an established operation is a move to a new location. But that's exactly what Bob Funking and William Stutler did with An Evening Dinner Theatre in Elmsford, New York. Funking carefully explained: "One of the key factors on which we based the decision to move was the fact that the new facility [could be seen from] our past location. There are dangers in having to re-educate patrons as to where you have relocated."

The new facility, which opened for business in February 1990, cost approximately $3.5 million; that included only the construction cost. Funking said, "In this location, construction costs are approximately $100 per square foot." Stutler and Funking's building totals over 32,000 square feet but houses only 450 patrons.

Funking's figures differ slightly from Turpin's:

Interior finish	$1,100,000
Equipment	925,000
Operating capital	535,000
Contingency fund	500,000
TOTAL	$3,060,000

Funking said that their equipment expenses ran between $300,000 and $400,000. The sound system cost $75,000 and the lighting system about $65,000. The performance and rehearsal decks alone cost in excess of $100,000. "Operating costs are higher in New York," Funking stated. His advertising and first-show costs doubled Turpin's figures. Funking also recommends that a theatre take whatever equipment, fixtures, and furniture it can from the old facility and transport it to the new location to cut costs. Also, stay as close as possible to the original location to maintain the current patrons.

An Evening Dinner Theatre changed its name to the Westchester Broadway Theatre, and Funking and Stutler were happy that the transition was a relatively smooth one.

CONTINUING THE OPERATION

Scott Griffith, owner of the 1,130-seat Carousel Dinner Theatre, who completed a successful shift from a location in Ravenna, Ohio, to a new facility in Akron, Ohio, has given some guidelines for operating costs. As president of the American Dinner Theatre Institute (ADTI), Griffith has collected these figures from the institute's member dinner theatres across the country:

Restaurant costs: costs of raw food, labor, supplies, and replacements. They depend on the area of the country and the type of food service, and range from $2.50 to $8.50 per person; variable costs.

Bar costs: costs of liquor, labor, supplies, and replacements. Liquor costs are generally 11–19 percent. Labor costs are 25 percent; supplies and replacements, 5 percent of sales.

Production costs: These vary widely, based on type of stage used, union or non-union status, use of star system, and elaborateness of shows; but they shouldn't be more than 33–35 percent of sales.

Overhead costs: These shouldn't be more than 30 percent of sales. This area includes advertising/promotions (6–9 percent); bank charges and bad debts; depreciation; dues, subscriptions, and licenses; insurance; interest expenses; maintenance and cleaning; office expenses, salaries, rents, and leases; repairs; legal and accounting fees; telephone and fax costs; taxes; and travel and entertainment.

These operating expenses will vary according to the theatre's location, the size of the theatre, its union or non-union status, its type of food service used, and type and size of productions. These figures can also be used as general guidelines for dinner theatres across the country.

Dollars Tell the Story

Even if a dinner theatre has spectacular and elaborate shows and serves the utmost in gourmet food, it's the dollars and cents—and how they're used—that keep an operation open. As demonstrated by many dinner theatres in the past, bankruptcy can be the final show if figures aren't carefully watched and strict budgets aren't maintained. Actors, directors, and staff have their respective roles within the operation, but it's ultimately the numbers that really tell the story.

Other costs for producers include fees for membership in professional associations such as the ADTI and the National Dinner Theatre Association (NDTA), and in the only professional stage actors union in the country—Actors' Equity Association.

ACTORS' EQUITY ASSOCIATION

The labor union that represents professional performers and stage managers in the legitimate theatre business throughout the United States is known as Actors' Equity Association (AEA). Founded in 1913, this organization negotiates working conditions for members, and minimum salaries, administers contracts, and enforces the provisions of the 20-odd national contracts with employers.

Actors' Equity Association, also known as Equity, is a branch of the Associated Actors and Artists of America, the organization that is affiliated with the AFL-CIO, from which all performer unions derive their jurisdictional charters.

Equity has been in the forefront on social issues, and, in its literature, states: "Actors' Equity has a proud history of fighting for social justice, beginning in 1947 with its refusal to allow Equity actors to perform at the then segregated National Theatre in Washington, D.C., and continuing today with its aggressive policy to help increase employment opportunities for ethnic minorities, women, and performers with disabilities. Equity was a sponsor of the first Symposium on Non-Traditional Casting held in New York in 1986, and continues its efforts to open the minds of producers, playwrights, and directors to the possibilities of non-traditional casting. Today, another ongoing effort in which Equity has taken the lead is the fight against AIDS and the social injustices suffered by those living with AIDS."

Equity reported that in 1990 the median annual earnings in theatre for an Equity actor were $4,934, and, at any given point, 80 percent of the union actors were not working. Those fortunate enough to find employment may be working in one of hundreds of theatres, including dinner theatres, across the country. To illustrate the transient nature of acting, Equity stated that an actor on a six-month bus-and-truck tour may travel nearly 20,000 miles and stay in 45 different hotel rooms. Also, to show the different theatre types included in Equity contracts, they reported that a typical small professional theatre has an *annual* operating budget of

$250,000. By contrast, a typical Broadway musical has a production budget of $5–6 million and a *weekly* operating budget of $300,000.

The largest national Equity contract is the Broadway contract. Then, in order, come the contracts for tours, LORT (League of Regional Theatres), small professional theatres, and dinner theatres. Contracts are based on number of actors' work weeks earned per year. There are a total of about 20 contracts with the AEA.

Aside from the many representational issues that Equity handles, there are some factors that are less desirable from the viewpoint of the producer or the actor. Whether to become an Equity-affiliated dinner theatre or, as an actor, to join the ranks of Equity depends on specific factors that differ for each locale and each individual.

UNION OR NON-UNION?

Dinner theatres fall basically into two categories: union (Equity-affili-ated theatres) or non-union (non-Equity affiliated). There are similarities and differences among these types of operations. It should be noted that the term "union" in this context refers to the actors' union and the supply of actors for dinner theatre productions.

Non-union dinner theatres have more flexibility in hiring, auditioning, and performances. Union dinner theatres are bound by the ADTI/AEA contract that closely regulates all of these areas. As a matter of fact, the contract is so lengthy that it is printed and bound in a booklet.

Union dinner theatres almost always pay talent a higher weekly salary than non-union theatres. This higher rate attracts the more seasoned performers along with the more-difficult-to-find, older character actors. In any case, there is a minimum scale that must be paid, based on theatre size.

Unlike the union dinner theatres, non-union dinner theatres normally do not contribute to pension funds for actors employed, nor do they usually pay for health insurance benefits for each actor. Being able to avoid these mandatory union costs allows the non-union theatres the opportunity to reinvest in other areas and achieve significant profits.

Employee security is one of the more prominent benefits a performer automatically gains by working for a union dinner theatre. Each union theatre, for example, must secure a bond covering actors' salaries in the event that a theatre closes for any reason.

Keep in mind that there are many quality union and non-union opera-tions throughout the country, where production values are exceptional, not to mention the level of food quality, service, and hospitality. Why, then, would a dinner theatre choose to be union-affiliated if the costs would be higher? There are several reasons why.

First, caliber of union talent is generally higher. Equity actors perform as a career, not as a hobby, as they do in community theatres. Non-union actors often hold other jobs for their main source of income.

Second, scheduling eight shows per week, including mid-week matinees, is often difficult for local actors even if their talent level is high. Almost always, then, local non-professional actors have other careers that provide their financial support.

Third, securing actors from the right age range, especially for certain character roles, is often extremely difficult. If a producer must find this talent in a predominantly non-union market, even though a non-union talent pool there may be large, it will still tend to lack in men and women able to portray middle-aged and elderly characters.

Finally, the Equity contract demands set times and procedures that producers can count on—summed up as professionalism. Inexperienced actors often need the time to learn the aspects of professionalism, and producers cannot afford to have actors who are not able to meet the rigid time and physical demands of the business.

Of course, there are fine non-Equity actors throughout the country. In fact, just because an actor has an Equity card does not mean that his or her talents automatically outshine those of a non-Equity performer. However, Equity status does have certain qualities associated with it that producers have learned to rely upon in casting and producing their shows. That talent commodity can be an invaluable asset to any quality dinner theatre, but with it go problems that must be weighed.

Pros and Cons of the Union Contract

One area that has seen change is the relationship between the Equity-affiliated dinner theatres and Equity. The pros and cons of the working agreement between the AEA and these dinner theatres are presented here, as discussed by producers and directors who are involved with talent on a day-to-day basis.

Hiring quality actors is an ongoing concern for dinner theatre producers. Not only talent, but professionalism, as well, is expected. Bill Stutler, producer for the Westchester Broadway Theatre in Elmsford, New York, is very pleased with the caliber of actors he hires, most of whom are members of Equity.

At this writing, there are 20 Equity dinner theatres throughout the country. They have what is known as a working agreement with the AEA.

This contract was negotiated in 1988 by the ADTI and the AEA; the AEA and the ADTI had negotiated and formulated the first dinner theatre contract of its kind in 1974. In May 1994, the current agreement will expire, and prior to the expiration, another set of negotiations will commence between the two organizations. It is estimated that the ADTI will spend in excess of $65,000 on negotiations to hopefully arrive at a mutually agreeable set of terms.

In a survey of ADTI producers, the issue found to be paramount in their minds is that of pension and welfare payments. It appears that the existence of pension and welfare payments is not the real issue; the escalating costs, especially of the weekly welfare contribution, have caused an alarming concern.

To best illustrate the average cost of hiring a principal Equity actor for a one-week period, figures are listed below for an actor in an AEA category IV dinner theatre as of January 1990:

Actor's salary	$397.00
Pension (8 percent)	31.76
Welfare (includes salary continuance)	62.64
Workmen's compensation	13.99
Federal unemployment tax	3.18
Employer's FICA	30.37
State unemployment tax	9.13
Total cost	$548.07

Thus, an actor's extra benefits cost the producer 38 percent of his/her salary, with the welfare portion making up 41 percent of this amount.

QUALITY TALENT IS EXPENSIVE

Tony D'Angelo, of the Candlelight Dinner Playhouse in Summit, Illinois, lists his costs on every Equity contract so that each actor can see what a producer must pay each week in addition to the actor's salary. D'Angelo feels that it's important to show talent these "blind costs."

Applying the old adage, "You get what you pay for," most Equity producers tend to accept the fact that most quality talent is expensive. Frank Wyka, a former producer for the now-defunct Grand Dinner Theatre in Anaheim, California, compared the Grand (which was Equity affiliated) to a non-union dinner theatre in the area and discovered that the non-Equity competitor tended to make more than twice as much gross profit because, in Wyka's opinion, the overwhelming talent costs he faced as a former AEA producer seriously cut into his profit margin. In Wyka's area, as well as in secondary markets, the talent pool of high-caliber non-union actors is building; and many producers are watching peripherally, as that pool grows.

D'Angelo says: "Equity actors are usually very professional. They're on time and understand rehearsal time frames. They're seasoned." One must keep in mind that working in an Equity dinner theatre means observing contractual stipulations governing work hours, rehearsal time, and overtime. Time *is* money.

Producer Doug Stark, of the Beef 'N Boards Dinner Theatre in Indianapolis, agrees that Equity performers offer not only experience, but also "age." Finding the older quality non-union character players is not easy. Stark also contends that most working actors don't utilize the welfare contribution, and most actors don't stay in the profession long enough to pull from the pension fund. However, Stark and D'Angelo agree that actors need insurance coverage. One suggestion made was that Equity allow the producer to provide insurance coverage by a private carrier. This would cover the actor for a six-month period, lowering the cost to the producer and perhaps providing better coverage for the performer.

Additional Costs

The cost of talent is also related to theatre size. Prescott F. Griffith, producer for, and owner of, the Carousel Dinner Theatre in Akron, brings in Broadway veterans for each show, to fill his 1,130-seat Equity house. Direct talent costs and fringe benefits are not the only financial burdens inherent in the AEA agreement. For instance, the Carousel is one of the few dinner theatres that regularly bring in the majority of its talent from New York City. Thus, Carousel must pay for actors' air fare (or the equivalent reimbursement for those who drive). A staggering $30,000 is spent each year by Griffith just for actors' transportation! One must consider other extra costs, such as that of required new dance shoes, for example, which can often exceed $2,500 per production.

"Our ticket prices are at the top of our price range; we just cannot afford to raise ticket prices commensurate with cost-of-living increases, taxes and talent costs that are quickly escalating," says Country Dinner's Bill McHale, who is feeling the same financial stress that producers and directors are experiencing across the country. "A 470-seat house was huge 20 years ago, but today that isn't so," McHale adds.

Working Toward a Solution

Solving this dilemma will not be easy. The AEA represents the talent. Of course, Equity wants the best wages and working conditions, along with continued employment, for its members. The producers want quality talent and to continuously employ top talent. The common denominator here is the desire to employ and the desire to be employed. Here, the actors are in the middle. If Equity, as well as the trustees of the Equity League Welfare Fund, work closely with producers to help cut costs to the point of allowing the potential of profitability during difficult economic times, both the AEA and the producers are accomplishing a basic goal: to keep quality talent employed.

Unfortunately, not all AEA members are aware of the cost factors plaguing many Equity producers. To complicate matters, actors are often under the misconception that all producers are incredibly wealthy and that the dinner theatre business is automatically an extremely high-profit industry. The "glitz and glamour" tend to mask the stark reality that rising theatre costs, coupled with higher royalty charges and skyrocketing talent costs, are setting the stage for a continuing loss of Equity dinner theatres.

The facts speak for themselves: In 1978 there were 78 Equity dinner theatres; in 1992 there are 20. Quality has its price, but is it a price that producers are able to pay?

Both the dinner theatre producers and the AEA must give serious consideration to supporting each other. If this does not happen, and the current pattern of Equity dinner theatres either closing or becoming non-Equity continues, then Agatha Christie may already have summed it up: "And then there were none."

ASSOCIATIONS FOR THE DINNER THEATRE INDUSTRY

To help producers in a variety of ways, there are two associations that work with dinner theatres across the country. These organizations are known as the National Dinner Theatre Association and the American Dinner Theatre Institute.

The National Dinner Theatre Association was organized in 1978 so that members could share varied perspectives on the dinner theatre industry. Members represent dinner theatres, mainly non-union, across the country. Their "Mission Statement" says: "Members represent some of the finest dinner theatres in the United States, from both the union and non-union sectors. They have joined together to share their experience and to plan for the future and to continue to explore methods and trends for increased standards of excellence in dinner theatre operations."

The primary function of the NDTA is to plan and present two annual conferences: one in the spring, which includes auditions; and one in the fall, which includes meetings and seminars but no auditions. Their membership includes approximately 29 dinner theatres and there is no paid representative on the staff.

American Dinner Theatre Institute

The American Dinner Theatre Institute is a trade association of professional dinner theatres stretching from the Pacific Coast to the East Coast.

The ADTI was founded at a conference of dinner theatre operators held in Dallas in October 1972. The main reason for the conference was to seek recognition for dinner theatres by negotiating an exclusive contract with Actors' Equity Association. At the time, dinner theatres were operating under various contracts negotiated with stock theatre managers' associations.

On August 28, 1972, Bob Boren had advised dinner theatre operators across the country that he and Willard Swire had had a meeting in Denver, one week earlier, attended also by Don Crute and Bill McHale. The purpose was to discuss a proposed dinner theatre contract with the AEA. Both Bob Boren and Josh Cockey then scheduled a meeting in Dallas for October 19-20, 1972.

Therefore, on October 19, 1972, the American Dinner Theatre Institute was born. Those attending the conference included Storer Boone (Beverly Dinner Theatre, New Orleans); Bob Boren (Country Dinner Playhouse, Denver); Josh Cockey (Limestone Valley Dinner Theatre, Cockeysville); Don Crute (Country Dinner Playhouse, Dallas); Ray Carlson (Colorado Music Hall, Denver); Ted Johnson (Alhambra Dinner Theatre, Jacksonville); Don McPherson (Beef 'N Boards, Louisville); Mike Hager (The Barn, Cedarcrest); Les Craver (Hayloft, Lubbock); Merrill Cohen (Avondale, Indianapolis); and Joe Stevens (The Barn, St. Louis).

Boren was elected president; a representative from Beef 'N Boards was elected vice president; Cockey was elected secretary; and Crute was elected treasurer.

Negotiations began with the AEA on March 14, 1973, and after four meetings in New York, they were completed on May 5, 1973. The first ADTI/AEA dinner theatre contract was ratified by members on May 14, 1973, in New Orleans; it was a one-year contract.

The second ADTI/Equity agreement was negotiated in the fall of 1974 and ratified on November 23, 1974. Since then, subsequent contracts have been negotiated, each with a duration of approximately three years.

From the first meeting of dinner theatre operators, it became apparent that a strong, active trade association would be of great value to the dinner theatre industry. In 1974 the first official ADTI executive secretary (now executive director) was hired and the ADTI opened its first office, in Dallas. The ADTI office was relocated to Sarasota, Florida, in 1979 and it remained there until the spring of 1987. It was then moved to Cockeysville, Maryland, for the following two years. In the fall of 1989, the ADTI made its next home-office relocation, to Akron, Ohio, with William M. Lynk as its executive director. The ADTI office acts as a clearinghouse for information on all phases of dinner theatre operations.

Since the ADTI is a trade association supported exclusively by membership dues from existing dinner theatres, its primary functions deal with operational rather than organizational procedures, but it does try to assist those people who are organizing new dinner theatres, in the hope that they will eventually become members.

The ADTI Constitution originally set forth its objectives as follows:

1. the advancement of improved construction, maintenance, management, and operation of professional year-round dinner theatres,
2. the promotion of and encouragement in maintaining good theatrical productions and wholesome food services,
3. the encouragement of free exchange of information and experience among its members and other competent and interested persons,
4. the promotion of a workable relationship with Actors' Equity Association.

Having obtained objective number four, and working agreements with the American Guild of Variety Artists and the Society of Stage Directors and Choreographers, the ADTI is now concentrating on its first three objectives. To that end, it has amended its constitution to permit the admission of all union dinner theatres as active members with Executive Board approval.

The ADTI attempts to determine the best and most efficient operating procedures and products available in order to recommend them to its members. In addition to a meeting held annually in various locations throughout the United States, it holds workshops focusing on such subjects as group sales, advertising and publicity, play production, and food trends. It is actively involved in investigating cost savings for the membership through any means possible.

The ADTI informs its members of new plays and musical productions that seem to have dinner theatre potential, and of revues, concerts, and other forms of entertainment that are suitable for dinner theatres. The ADTI also publishes a monthly newsletter that has carried articles on many applicable topics.

The executive director (this writer) has a regular column in *Back Stage*. The column, entitled "Dinner Theatre Scenes," focuses on information pertinent to the dinner theatre industry. By exchanging information and operating procedures, the ADTI hopes to be able to lower costs for its members without sacrificing quality, and to improve the overall standards of the dinner theatre industry.

CHANGES ON THE EAST COAST

Changes can be either good or bad, depending on the situation. For the Darien Dinner Theatre, it was a change in management that completely turned the theatre around. The section below illustrates the importance of quality management in running a profitable and successful dinner theatre.

From the Beginning

In the autumn months of 1977, construction was completed on a building in Darien, in southern Connecticut. Designed and built from the ground up, the Darien Dinner Theatre has operated continuously for 52 weeks per year and is the only Equity dinner theatre in the state of Connecticut.

The theatre was built and owned by John Grogan, Michael Minihan, and a small group of investors. Originally, the idea was conceived that a Broadway director, Morton DaCosta, would be the resident director, and so the theatre and concept were designed for him. Shows would originate in Darien and move on to other dinner theatres that would be built in similar fashion. Unfortunately, this concept never materialized.

"High Spirits" were not only the feelings during the opening in 1977, but also the name of the Broadway show that opened the Darien Dinner Theatre. The show was directed by Morton DaCosta and starred Jan Miner and Ellen Hanley. But other parts of the operation were certainly unsettled. There was no curtain, the food was poor, the plumbing was unfinished, employees were not paid, and many seats remained unfilled in the 399-seat Equity theatre. Tough financial times ensued and the operation was then taken over by new owners in 1984. One year later, new management took the helm.

Running the Ship

Indeed, the executive producer and chief operating officer, Jane Bergere, has made numerous changes since her appointment in 1985, breathing new life into a failing operation. Bergere gradually turned the theatre into a ship-shape operation.

Jane Bergere has been involved in theatre all her life. Once an aspiring pianist, Bergere also played cello and harp and won the Metropolitan Opera regional auditions at the age of 16. One of the judges suggested that she enroll in the program of the renowned Opera Department at Indiana University. She did, and graduated with a major in music and a minor in speech and theatre.

After playing her role in the national company of *Camelot*, Jane became convinced that she loved musical comedy, and she then did featured roles in the Broadway and regional productions of *Fiddler on the Roof*, *Company*, *West Side Story*, *Mame*, and *Guys and Dolls*. She has also appeared on such soaps as "The Guiding Light," "The Doctors," and "As the World Turns." While working in the theatre, Jane was also selling real estate. She helped launch the residential department of the Cross & Brown Company in New York and chalked up record real estate sales during her tenure.

Combining two of her talents—theatre and business—Bergere just wouldn't sit back and ride the wave. She explained: "Right now I find I spend 16 hours a day, seven days a week, at the theatre. I think that in order to do one thing well, you have to devote yourself to it." When asked about her hectic schedule, Bergere commented: "I think work is very healthy for people. It keeps your mind tuned and gives you enlightenment on life."

During Bergere's first three years at the theatre, 120,000 patrons per year attended productions that garnered rave reviews. This attendance represented a 25 percent increase from what it had been.

Modifying the Facility

One of Bergere's additions included the use of a new turntable stage that premiered during a run of *Guys and Dolls*, her first directed production at the Darien facility. This turntable allowed her to contrast the vastness of New York stages with the intimacy of scenes in the show and in their theatre. Other alterations that followed included banners designed by the award-winning James Tilton, which enhanced the sound as well as the look of the theatre. Colors, wall hangings, and table settings were also improved.

One major change that was immediately implemented upon Bergere's arrival was the conversion from "dreary cafeteria food" to an attractively presented and appetizing buffet meal. Then, Bergere went a step further and created an elegant table service menu that included prime rib of beef, chicken marsala, fresh filet of sole with shrimp and seafood stuffing, and chicken paillard for health-conscious patrons. "To do it right," Bergere asserts, "one has to love theatre and food and I have a passion for both!"

Her Goal

When asked what her main goal is, Bergere answered: "The American musical is something very unique. It's an important part of our culture, of Americana, and must be kept alive." With that in mind, she said: "I see the reality of making this theatre [her theatre] the jewel of Fairfield County." She is doing this by good management and by her accessibility: "I am accessible to everybody in the company, [to] the staff, and all of our guests. We are in a service business, and what's most important is that good service be given in every area. I like to think of this dinner theatre as a total experience: 'Come, park your car, have good food, entertainment, and leave feeling better than when you came in.' I want people to know that they can have a wonderful evening and don't have to go to New York to do it."

Her Many Roles

Along with her directing, Bergere also supervises the 125 employees, and coordinates the sets, lighting, cast, crew, orchestra, sound technicians, directors, and choreographers. She oversees every production, supervises the restaurant operation, approves menus, and oversees the facility, ticket sales, and guest relations problems.

And, then, she has family responsibilities. Bergere explains her success: "I'm very fortunate. I have a saint of a husband, a wonderful teenage daughter, an adorable four-year-old; a very understanding and loving family." Thinking back five years, Jane recalls: "I was in a euphoric state of pregnancy. I was oblivious to what bad shape the theatre was in, and maybe when you're pregnant, you think you can do anything. I went into labor on my way to the theatre and realized I better go to the hospital instead."

She and her husband and children live in Manhattan, and Jane commutes daily. As a busy woman, taking on the roles of a mother and wife, a real estate agent, a notary, the first vice president of the American Dinner

Theatre Institute, and an executive producer, her hard work and dedication were cited when she won the 1990 Westchester County Woman of the Year Award for outstanding achievement in and contribution to the theatre. Some of the past recipients have included such notables as Shirley Temple Black, Celeste Holm, Gloria Vanderbilt, Kitty Carlisle Hart, the late Colleen Dewhurst, and Jeanne Kirkpatrick.

To better represent (to the public) what her theatre is all about, Bergere changed the name of the Darien Dinner Theatre to Connecticut's Broadway Theatre. Obviously her dedication and focus have helped to turn a floundering dinner theatre into a quality operation. As Jane Bergere continues to display her love and passion for the theatre, so, too, will she promote her dream—the continuation of the American musical theatre.

PROBLEMS OBTAINING A SHOW

Producers argue that problems arise in a competitive market when two dinner theatres, or any number of theatres, for that matter, produce the same show at the same time, back to back or in an overlapping manner. These producers, along with many other professional and amateur producers, often wonder what would happen if the royalty houses that license these shows were to restrict productions to alleviate conflicts. Representatives of the royalty houses feel, however, that restrictions of this nature would not be in either party's best interests. And if such licensing restrictions were implemented, based on geographic areas, how would this mechanism be established to ensure and promote fairness?

Restrictions, Please

One of these instances of simultaneous licensing reportedly occurred in Kansas City. The show *Lend Me a Tenor* was licensed to both Tiffany's Attic Dinner Theatre and the American Heartland Dinner Theatre, both Equity-affiliated houses.

Dennis Hennessy, co-owner of Tiffany's Attic, said of this coincidence: "It has tremendously affected our theatre." Hennessy explained that because his competitor produced *Lend Me a Tenor* just after Tiffany's production had closed, he discovered that his audience members who would have attended felt they could wait to see the show at a later date. Obviously, individual ticket sales are affected in this scenario. "It leads to a confused market; audiences are confused as to where the show will be playing," adds Hennessy.

Other problems existed as well. Hennessy feels that their competitor was "hanging on their coattails" with regard to the residual effect of Tiffany's advertising. Hennessy's marketing techniques and promotions in effect benefited the competitor while he lost ticket sales during his own run.

Even though the American Heartland opened its version of *Lend Me a Tenor* after Tiffany's production, Lilli Zarda, Tiffany's general manager, feels that it isn't a good situation: "In a small community like Kansas City, with only 1.5 million people, this type of simultaneous run could have an adverse effect on a for-profit operation."

It turns out that each theatre was aware, at the time of the signing, that the other was interested in the show. One, then, may ask, "Why didn't one of the theatres drop the show from its list?" Zarda explained that choosing *Tenor* was necessary because it was "the best show for the time slot." Zarda also explained that they extended *Ain't Misbehavin'* because of its over-whelming popularity and because it would help alleviate the overlap conflict. She stated: "It was not selected for any competitive reason. It was a simultaneous decision by both theatres." Both theatres do agree that changing a season schedule at the last minute is difficult, at best, especially when arrangements are being made for actors, props, costumes, and scenery. Zarda also feels that the royalty house, in this case Samuel French, should employ a restriction clause to avert this type of situation in the future. But the royalty houses didn't tend to agree.

Open to All—Almost

The royalty houses represent the authors of various plays and musicals that they license. "We do our best to protect professional companies, but it is the individual theatre's responsibility to work out conflicts," says Robert Vaughan, a 10-year veteran in the professional department of the Samuel French Company. He adds: "We really can't monitor professional companies; we just can't do it. Usually the theatres in large metropolitan cities tend to work well together. They work things out." Dennis Hennessy quickly responds to that statement: "It's nice to say that, but if theatres who are highly competitive are not cooperating, it certainly hurts. Samuel French Company has always been very fair to us in the past, but we think they have a responsibility here."

Vaughan explains that exclusivities are granted to professional compa-nies when, for example, a non-professional company in a city wants to produce a show at the same time that a professional company in the same city is scheduled (licensed) for that show. Vaughan said that they will try to alert other producers if they are aware that they have licensed a particular show, but among professional companies, there are no restrictions or exclusive rights based on geography. He says, "We're on a first-come, first-serve basis."

Following a similar philosophy is Music Theatre International (MTI). Richard Salfas, director of the company's dinner theatre department, stated: "The only time we would grant exclusivity is if a major tour is coming through an area; for example, the *Fiddler on the Roof* tour. Also, we may consider a major regional production." When asked if restrictions would be placed on use of shows by professional and non-professional companies, Salfas responded: "We'd think about it." He then added: "We try our best to keep track of what's happening with our shows." He said that MTI uses a computer system that allows them to scan a particular area of the screen. He also stated that MTI tries to make clients aware if a potential conflict might arise. "We like to be fair and honest," he added.

But what constitutes "fair" in cases dealing especially with hot properties, on which producers want to purchase the rights? Could a system of exclusivities really operate equally and fairly?

Hennessy readily admitted that such a system could work against the producers as easily as it could work for them. If theatres in the same market had to bid for a show they were interested in producing, would bidding wars result? If so, then only the larger theatres would probably win, most often to the detriment of the smaller theatres, especially since high-quality new shows for the dinner theatre circuit are currently at a low ebb. Could such a system be created by use of a "letter of intent" from the producer to the royalty house, based on the date of the letter's receipt? This, too, could create a mountain of paperwork that might be difficult to process. Zarda feels that the current royalty percentages are already sky-high and a bidding structure would only act to raise the royalties to the point of unaffordability. Zarda says, "Most theatres are facing difficult economic times." Zarda added that the royalty houses need to work with the theatres so that they are not compounding the problem, especially in light of the narrow profit margin of most dinner theatres.

Both MTI and Samuel French feel that exclusivity restrictions are not the answer. Salfas gave an example of a conflict that occurred between a college and a community theatre, both licensed to produce *Into the Woods* at the same time in the same area. They ended up doing a joint production that turned out to be wonderful, according to Salfas. Not all conflicts, though, can be resolved that easily.

If, in fact, the royalty houses were representing the authors, exclusivity restrictions would only act to limit the amount of productions possible, and thus, the amount of income both the authors and royalty houses could ultimately realize.

No Simple Answer

After evaluating all the options, Dennis Hennessy concluded that bidding wars could devastate smaller theatres. Also, producers are voicing the concern that royalties already are too high.

Luckily, Zarda stated, the American Heartland hadn't been adversely affected by conflicts, because of their strong subscriber base and heavy group sales. She also said that if their theatre depended on single-ticket sales, they'd be in serious trouble because of the two area productions of *Lend Me a Tenor.*

Hennessy said that this situation has occurred three times in his market. He noted: "If another theatre announces a show we plan to do, we will drop it from our schedule. But, it certainly makes it difficult to advance-plan a season."

Royalty houses say that conflicts of this sort between theatres are very minimal, and when they do exist, theatres work them out themselves. But as can be seen here, it isn't always that simple.

The adage, "Don't rock the boat" may be aptly used here. Restrictions may cause more problems than the ones they alleviate.

Unless the producers go more toward new and experimental works (as some theatres are attempting to do, with mixed results), the royalty houses will continue to dominate theatres choosing to pay, and sometimes dearly, for the privilege of producing a select play or musical.

MARKETING IDEAS FOR DINNER THEATRE

In most locales, summer and winter can be slow periods in the dinner theatre industry. During these times, even more effort needs to be expended in the area of promotions in order to compensate for lower levels of ticket sales that occur.

One excellent example of this took place during a summer production in the Midwest. The Carousel Dinner Theatre in Akron made a major commitment to the National Rock 'N' Roll Hall of Fame and Museum (RRHF), in Cleveland, the nation's official home for rock 'n' roll. To help offset the $41 million still needed for financing in 1991, the Carousel's owner, Prescott F. Griffith, and its director of public relations and advertising, Betty Wilson, formulated a promotional campaign, in cooperation with area radio stations, whereby a portion of ticket receipts as contributed to aid the cause. And the show chosen for the campaign was none other than *Grease*, the rollicking and beebopping show based on the late 1950s.

In order to create an awareness of the Carousel Dinner Theatre and the Rock 'N' Roll Hall of Fame, joint efforts were made. Betty Wilson was very excited about the *Grease* promotions. Ms. Wilson said, "Regional radio stations joined forces with the Carousel to help raise awareness and funds for the RRHF. Tying in with radio stations has tremendous public relations value, not just for the RRHF, but for Carousel and the dinner theatre industry." Wilson said that *Grease* is an ideal show for introducing younger audiences to the dinner theatre experience: "With *Grease* and the RRHF promo tie-in, we've opened the doors to radio stations whose format targets the younger audiences. Not only did this raise the level of awareness for *Grease*, but we've certainly invested in our future—the younger market.

"Many of the stations invited our New York cast to appear on their drive-time shows. It was a wonderful tie-in. Not only was the show a fun production, but the extra promotions, such as contests, sock hops, and on-air promos, added to the excitement."

Wilson certainly had her hands full, especially since she appeared on many of the stations plugging the show and the talented cast. She even worked out details that gave the cast the honor of singing the National Anthem at a Cleveland Indians baseball game in August during the show's run. With 15 years in the advertising and public relations field, Wilson has thought up and instituted literally hundreds of clever, and ultimately profitable, eye- and ear-appealing gimmicks. Here's a perfect example of how one sound promotional idea led beautifully to others that were all interrelated in an effort to advertise more than just a production.

Wilson recalled some marketing ideas that she used during the 1992 production of *Little Shop of Horrors*. "January is traditionally a slow time for us, so we brainstormed a variety of creative promotional ideas that would tie in to the show. We even announced that a $100 cash prize could be awarded to a staff member who could come up with an effective promotion that we could use. It turned out being a cast member, Ron Ransen, who thought up [a] 'Feed the Plant' promotion." A local high-power radio station agreed to promote "Feed the Plant" by asking listeners to call in and state why they felt they should be "fed to the plant." During a five-day period, one caller daily would win dinner and show tickets for two. After the performance, the winner would be literally fed to the people-eating plant from the show. A Polaroid photo would be given as a keepsake. The promotion worked wonderfully and helped raise ticket sales considerably.

100 Trombones?

Many consider the Chanhassen Dinner Theatres, in Minnesota, to be unique, in that they are actually three different theatres under one roof: the Main Dinner Theatre, which seats 590; the Fireside, seating 290; and the Playhouse, which seats 190. A fourth theatre, the Courtyard, alternates with the Playhouse in doing various productions.

During a production of *The Music Man*, a promotion was created to add excitement and draw attention; an ensemble of 100 trombones opened the show at the premiere. Kris Howland, public relations manager for the Chanhassen Theatres, stated that about 60 percent of the volunteers were from either high schools or colleges. Why not 76 instead of 100? Over 200 had called to volunteer and space limitations would allow only 100. Howland felt the promotion was a great success.

Presented below is a marketing plan, as used by the Carousel Dinner Theatre for a production of *The Music Man*, starring George Chakiris. By reviewing an actual plan, producers and marketing directors may gain additional ideas that can be applied to other productions.

MARKETING PLAN

For: *The Music Man*—August 29–October 21, 1990,
Carousel Dinner Theatre
Created by: Betty Wilson, Director of Public Relations and Advertising

TARGET MARKET

The major market is the 35-and-over group, which cherishes classic musical theatre. Also included in this target market are young families looking for wholesome and affordable family entertainment, theatre lovers (all ages) who enjoy the classic musicals, students (high school and college), band members and theatre majors who have performed in *The Music Man* in various productions, and the Greek community tieing into George Chakiris (star of the show).

TOTAL CONCEPT

Great all-American music, upbeat, lively high-energy music; classic musical theatre with broad appeal to musical theatre lovers of all ages, not limited to, but concentrating on, the above-stated target market; development of promotional aspects dealing with "band musicians, barbershop quartets, and libraries."

LOOK AND FEEL

The look and feel of all material should be brassy with an all-American feel associated with it, utilizing a red, white, and blue color scheme. Musical symbols and instruments should also be used, not overlooking the star, George Chakiris.

ADVERTISING METHODS

Use radio, newspapers, print support, television, and promotions.

PROMOTIONS FOR SHOW

1. "76 Trombones or 110 Cornets": Make calls to local high schools, colleges, musicians' unions, music stores, and churches to secure volunteers to perform on gala opening night, in exchange for show-only tickets and media opportunity. Set rehearsal and performance times and guidelines.

2. Family Night: Co-promote with radio station (WAKR or WKDD in Akron, and WDOK in Cleveland); total promotion through radio station as co-promoter of the official Family Night at the Carousel. Patrons can buy one full-price adult ticket, and child is admitted free, with children's menu. Implement on Tuesday nights during the show's run.

3. Barbershop quartets: Contact local BQs, have them serenade guests as they dine, for approximately one-half hour. Quartets will stroll through the theatre in special outfits as they perform. Check with the Akron and Cleveland chapters of SPEBSQSA (Society for the Preservation and Encouragement of Barbershop Quartet Singing in America) to secure a quartet for each of the eight weeks. Investigate the idea of volunteers, in exchange for dinner and show tickets. Check logistics of microphones.

4. Singles 'n stars club: Set dates for either the second or third Saturday night, in conjunction with theatre ticket counts.

5. Library tie-in: Develop a library tie-in with Akron, Canton, and Cleveland public libraries to incorporate a "library" aspect of a show. Gimmick/hook: present a library card for special incentive, discount, dessert, etc.

6. Banjo contest: Establish a banjo competition at the theatre, or, have banjo players entertain during dinner. Possible tie-in with sing-along.

FUND RAISERS

1. Develop a high school band fund raiser.

2. Contact, and set up chapter fund raiser with, sales and marketing executives (tie in with salesman theme).

3. Fund-raiser possibilities with SPEBSQSA (barbershop quartets).

OPENING WEEK/PRESS NIGHT

1. Invitations: Drop by on Monday, August 10, or Wednesday, August 12, at the latest. Incorporate "76 Trombones" score screened under an invitation copy with Chakiris's photo. Attach small (cocktail-size) paper American flag to insert into invitation. Mail media invitation to 185 newspaper/radio/theatre reviewers, announcing show and information on Press Night. This is a clever, unusual, and inexpensive piece.

2. Press name tags: Incorporate small, plastic brass-painted instruments into name tag.

3. Intermission gimmick: Prepare a plastic library card saying: "Check out the cast upstairs after the show." Call library for "rejects."

4. Other gimmicks: 76 trombones playing after pre-show; ice cream social at press party with barbershop quartet or banjo player as entertainment.

5. Cast gift: plastic, squeeze drink bottles with Carousel/*Music Man* logos imprinted.

MEDIA INFORMATION/TIMETABLE

Press release schedule: Chakiris announcement—drop in mail late on Friday, July 27; show release with Press Night invitation—drop late on Friday, August 10; release about 76 tromboners, with photo opportunity—drop late on Friday, August 17.

George Chakiris interview schedule: Television—"Morning Exchange"; "Live on Five"; "First Report"; "Lanigan Prize Movie." Radio—WMJI; WAKR; WERE; WNIR; WRMR.

Ticket giveaways: For Wednesday, August 29, for "Morning Exchange"; for WAKR; WDOK; WRMR; WNIR; WMJI; WKDD; WQMX; WQAL; WHBC.

Radio Advertising Plan

Scheduled budget: $6,000, with $500 for creation.

Commercial concept: Brassy, all-American musical spot highlighting musical excitement, and family oriented; highlighting Academy Award winner George

Chakiris; John Philip Sousa-sounding. Spot opens with background marching music; announcer is a fast-talking salesman (similar to Federal Express commercials).

Stations: those marketing to a 35-and-over age range, plus young-family market of WAKR (spots to use in trade), WNIR, WDOK, WRMR, WHBC, WKBN, and possibly WQAL.

Newspaper Advertising Plan

Scheduled budget: $19,000

Newspapers: Akron *Beacon Journal*; Cleveland *Plain Dealer*; Canton *Repository*; Youngstown *Vindicator*, *Record Courier*. Schedule starts as part of the ads for the McGuire Sisters; major boost—Friday, August 17. Ads range in size— 2" × 3", 2" × 6", 2" × 5", and 1" × 5", designed so one can insert special boxes for show events.

Print Support

Media invitations: These are as previously discussed.

Target mailings: Develop a piece (brassy/all-American) promoting the show and George Chakiris. Send 5,000 pieces to arrive in homes by Monday, August 20, and dropped in mailboxes by Friday, August 17. Additional pieces can be printed and placed at tables for the remainder of *Hello, Dolly!* run. This piece can be used as a poster in high schools and music stores. Size will be 11" × 17" on two-color glossy stock.

CHAPTER 6

Profiles of Selected Dinner Theatres

Alhambra Dinner Theatre
12000 Beach Blvd.
Jacksonville, FL 32216

Opening date: October 1967	Equity/non-Equity: Equity
Number on staff: 125	Ticket price range: $22.50–27.50
Population of area (50 mi.): 1 million plus	Seating capacity: 400
Productions per year: 7	Average length of runs: 8 weeks
Buffet/table service: buffet	Stage type: thrust
Box office: (904) 641-1212	Owner: Tod Booth

Locale: Jacksonville is part of a large geographic area (855 square miles) housing a population of over one million within a one-hour drive. The Alhambra is the only professional dinner theatre in the area. The largely middle-income populace has most occupations in the white-collar sector of the service industries. Jacksonville accommodates four naval bases that help in the local economy.

History: The Alhambra was originally owned by Leon Simon. In December 1985 Tod Booth Productions took over ownership. Sales in 1990 were $1 million and increased to $2.5 million in 1991.

Staff: Tod Booth, Owner
Greg Infante, Director of Sales
Steven Osborn, Director of Marketing and Advertising
Robert W. Rupp, Art Director; Assistant Producer

William Trent, Business Manager
Barbara Roll, Comptroller

Tod Booth (Owner) has directed over 200 productions during a career spanning over 30 years. Although he began his career as an actor, he has kept busy in all areas of theatre. He has appeared opposite such notables as Shelly Winters, Nanette Fabray, Claude Akins, Dan O'Herlihy, Mickey Rooney, and Ann Jillian. His directing credits include productions starring Lana Turner, Cloris Leachman, Robert Conrad, Ray Walston, Frank Gorshin, Vera Miles, Elke Sommer, Cesar Romero, Chuck Connors, and many more.

Comments: The Alhambra Dinner Theatre, the Alhambra Scenery Shop, and Tod Booth Advertising are wholly owned subsidiaries of Tod Booth Productions, Inc. The facility and property are owned by Alhambra Associates, Tod Booth, and Lisa Valdini Booth. The Alhambra Scenery Shop provides sets and costumes for major films and network television productions, and theme party sets for resorts.

Ascot Dinner Theatre
9136 West Bowles Ave.
Littleton, CO 80123

Opening date: March 1990

Number on staff: 135

Population of area (50 mi.): 1,900,000

Productions per year: 6

Buffet/table service: table

Box office: (303) 971-0100

Equity/non-Equity: non-Equity

Ticket price range: $16–30

Seating capacity: 629

Average length of runs: 8 weeks

Stage type: proscenium

Owner: Dinner Theatre Holdings, Ltd.

Locale: The Ascot is housed in 35,000 square feet of leasehold space in an upscale/retail center in southwest suburban Denver. The surrounding area is primarily mid-to-upscale residential. Two-thirds of the adults in the metro Denver area can drive to the Ascot in 30 minutes.

History: After eight years in the planning stage, the Ascot opened in March 1990. The ownership of the theatre has remained essentially the same throughout the planning, construction, and inaugural phases.

Staff: Dinner Theatre Holdings, Ltd., Owner
Mark Turpin, Executive Producer/Managing Partner
Carole A. Shear, Director of Business Services
William Miller, Director of Food and Beverages
Donna B. McDonald, Sales Manager
Curt Olson, Advertising Manager
Rod A. Lansberry, Production Manager

Comments: The Ascot is considered by many to be the epitome of dinner theatre elegance in Colorado. Its size and extensive production facilities allow for major productions of Broadway musicals and comedies, equal to those of the finest touring companies.

Beef 'N Boards Dinner Theatre
9301 N. Michigan Rd.
Indianapolis, IN 46268

Opening date: March 1972	Equity/non-Equity: Equity
Number on staff: 80	Ticket price range: $17.50–29.50
Population of area (50 mi.): 2 million	Seating capacity: 500
Productions per year: 6	Average length of runs: 8–10 weeks
Buffet/table service: buffet	Stage type: thrust
Box office: (317) 872-9664	Owners: Douglas Stark and Bob Zehr

Locale: The Beef 'N Boards Dinner Theatre is located in the northwest corner of I-465. Take the Michigan Road exit and proceed behind the Holiday Inn in the College Park-Pyramid area.

Staff: Douglas Stark, Owner/Producer
Bob Zehr, Owner/Producer
Amy Jo Stark, Public Relations
Peggy Zehr, Assistant to Producers
Sally Ashley, Group Sales
Pat Minneman, Group Sales
Ed Stockman, Stage Manager
Odell Ward, Chef
David McGregor, Service Manager

Comments: Beef 'N Boards has been under the current ownership for the past 12 years and remains Indiana's only year-round Equity dinner theatre.

Boulder's Dinner Theatre
5501 Arapahoe
Boulder, CO 80303

Opening date: 1977	Equity/non-Equity: non-Equity
Number on staff: 95	Ticket price range: $20–31
Population of area (50 mi.): 1.5 million	Seating capacity: 290
Productions per year: 3–4	Average length of runs: 4 months
Buffet/table service: table	Stage type: thrust (3/4)
Box office: (303) 449-6000	Owners: Ross Haley, Jody Sarbaugh, Doug McLemore

Locale: Nestled in the Colorado foothills, Boulder's Dinner Theatre is located in picturesque Boulder, home of the University of Colorado and the Boulder Mall. Boulder is only 25 miles from downtown Denver and the drive to Boulder gives one a panoramic view of the Rockies. The climate is temperate—cool summer evenings but winter temperatures often reaching 65 degrees.

Staff: Ross Haley, General Manager/Director/Owner
        Jody Sarbaugh, Producer/Owner
        Doug McLemore, Comptroller/Owner
        Tim McDonough, Food and Beverage Manager
        Misti Kelsay, Dining Room Supervisor/Lighting Design
        Rick Stone, Technical Director
        Jackie Cooney, Group Marketing Manager
        Scott Beyette, Co-director
        D. P. Perkins, Production Manager

Boulder's Dinner Theatre won six Denver Critics Circle awards in 1991 for its four-month run of *Chess*. Awards in fact are won every year by Boulder's Dinner Theatre, but 1991 brought a record number for *Chess*, including Best Musical, Best Director, Best Actor, Best Supporting Actor, and Best Costumes.

Comments: The year-round theatre is open six days per week with two performances on Sunday. The theatre is dark on Monday.

Burn Brae Dinner Theatre
3811 Blackburn Lane
Burtonsville, MD 20866

Opening date: May 1968	Equity/non-Equity: non-Equity
Number on staff: 40	Ticket price range: $24–30
Population of area (50 mi.): 1.5 million	Seating capacity: 400
Productions per year: 4	Average length of runs: 14 weeks
Buffet/table service: buffet	Stage type: thrust
Box office: (301) 384-5800	Owner: John Kinnamon

Locale: Burn Brae is located on Route 29, midway between Washington, D.C., and Baltimore, Maryland.

History: Burn Brae was the first dinner theatre in the Washington, D.C., market when it opened in May 1968. Since then, three major expansions have taken place.

Staff: John Kinnamon, Owner
        John Sichina, General Manager
        Sarah O'Leary, Day Manager
        Barbara Turek, Box Office Manager/Group Sales

Anna Siminski, Director of Group Sales
Donna Breed Love, Chef

John Kinnamon, owner of the Burn Brae Dinner Theatre, is a former producer/ director for NBC-TV and was a tenor soloist with Arthur Fiedler and the Boston Pops during 1970–73. Over 200 performers from Burn Brae have gone on to Broadway and to films.

Candlelight Dinner Playhouse
5620 South Harlem Ave.
Summit, IL 60501

Opening date: July 7, 1961	Equity/non-Equity: Equity
Number on staff: 200	Ticket price range: $29.95–41.95
Population of area (50 mi.): 9 million	Seating capacity: 550
Productions per year: 4	Average length of runs: 13 weeks
Buffet/table service: table	Stage type: arena-hydraulic lift
Box office: (708) 496-3000	Owner: William Pullinsi

Locale: Summit, Illinois, is a near-southwest suburb of Chicago. A working-class neighborhood, Summit is a small and supportive community. The Candlelight is located just 15 minutes from downtown Chicago, via the Stevenson Expressway (I-55 South), on South Harlem Avenue.

History: Bill Pullinsi decided to open a summer theatre when he was a freshman at Catholic University in Washington, D.C. With a classmate, Tony D'Angelo, and the financial backing of his grandfather, William Altier, Pullinsi opened the Candlelight Dinner Playhouse in July of 1959, becoming owner of America's first dinner theatre. On July 7, 1961, they opened in Chicago in a converted building that Bill's grandfather owned. In 1964 a specially designed theatre was built; in 1966 they expanded the seating to 550. They built the Forum Theatre next door in 1972 to present European and American plays. In 1992, a major renovation took place at the Candlelight and the Forum was converted into a dinner theatre, as well.

Staff: William Pullinsi, Owner/Artistic Director
Tony D'Angelo, Owner/Managing Director
Dennis Conway, General Manager
Eileen LaCario, Marketing Director

William Pullinsi originated the dinner theatre concept with the opening of the Candlelight in 1959. The Joseph Jefferson Committee (of Chicago) presented to Pullinsi a special Jefferson Award for "many years of innovation and quality, bringing the joys of live theatre to hundreds of thousands of Chicago-area patrons." He has directed every type of show—musicals, comedies, and dramas—and has received more than 20 Jefferson Award nominations and 14 Jefferson Awards for excellence in direction and production. Pullinsi received his BFA degree at the Boston Conservatory and did graduate work at the Goodman School. He received the honorary degree of doctor of humanities from Lewis University (Lockport, Illinois), and was honored as a distinguished artist in the theatre by the Chicago Academy for the Arts. In December of 1989, Pullinsi became the first American director to stage a musical in Russia with a Soviet cast and crew.

Anthony D'Angelo has been associated with the Candlelight since its inception in 1959. His settings and technical excellence have won him Best Production awards from the Jefferson Awards Committee. D'Angelo has contributed many of the theatrical innovations incorporated into the Forum Theatre and the Candlelight Playhouse, including Candlelight's much-acclaimed mechanical stage. His background ranges from art and literature to electrical engineering.

Comments: Prior to the Candlelight's opening, there were very few professionally produced local plays. No Chicago company ran 52 weeks per year, no show ran longer than three weeks, and no theatre operated successfully without the star system. Candlelight's success greatly influenced other theatre companies throughout the country. Through the dinner theatre format, Pullinsi and his company introduced great numbers of people to live theatre who traditionally had not attended.

Carousel Dinner Theatre
1275 East Waterloo Rd.
P.O. Box 7530
Akron, OH 44306

Opening date: April 1973	Equity/non-Equity: Equity
Number on staff: 175	Ticket price range: $23.50–31.00
Population of area (50 mi.): 4 million	Seating capacity: 1,130
Productions per year: 6–8	Average length of runs: 6–8 weeks
Buffet/table service: table	Stage type: proscenium
Box office: (216) 724-9855	Owner: Prescott F. Griffith

Locale: The Carousel is located in Akron, approximately 25 miles south of Cleveland. The theatre is situated just off the Kelly Road exit on Route 224 and I-77.

History: The largest professional dinner theatre in the country and the only professional dinner theatre in Ohio, the Carousel combines the atmosphere of a luxurious New York City supper club of the 1940s and the glamour of a Las Vegas showroom.

The Carousel Dinner Theatre began operations in 1973 in a converted Ravenna, Ohio, supermarket. Currently owned and operated by Prescott F.

Griffith, who assumed management of the theatre in 1978, the Carousel moved to the current Akron facility, at 1275 East Waterloo Road, in March 1988. With 51,000 square feet, the Carousel can entertain over 1,000 guests. The state-of-the-art sound and lighting complements the beautiful and intimate proscenium thrust stage. The operation also includes a separate banquet facility suitable for private parties, featuring a private balcony from which to view the show.

Nationally recognized as the epitome of first-class dining, decor, and entertainment, the Carousel regularly entertains dinner theatre owners from across the country. Currently, Prescott Griffith is the elected president of the American Dinner Theatre Institute, the national organization of professional dinner theatre owners and operators.

Specifically designed for the comfort and pleasure of its guests, the Carousel offers free parking for over 1,000 cars and a separate motorcoach port and a group entrance. Conveniently located restrooms and accessibility for the handicapped are ensured throughout. Also provided is a large permanent non-smoking section.

The state of Ohio, as well as the Akron community, have welcomed the Carousel as a vital force for tourism, citing its proven track record of group-tour business from all over the country and Canada, and from international travelers.

Staff: Prescott F. Griffith, Owner/Executive Producer
Marc Resnik, Associate Producer
Lisa Spiker, Director of Administration
Marque Sandrock, Director of Operations
Betty Wilson, Director of Public Relations/Advertising
Virginia Kancler, Director of Group Sales

Prescott F. Griffith, a native of Ft. Dodge, Iowa, and the son of an architect, displayed his first interest in theatre in high school, acting in, then producing, shows. He left such a mark on the school that its annual award to the outstanding student in theatre was named for him. As a student at Drake University, while completing his BS degree in accounting, Griffith assembled a theatre company to perform Broadway musicals during the winter in restaurants throughout Iowa, and during the summer at the Tabor Opera House in Leadville, Colorado. He also was chosen as the first director of student and faculty computing at the then new Dial Computer Center at Drake. He moved to Minneapolis to earn a master's degree in management information systems (MIS) though continuing to operate his theatrical company and to act as consultant, in the MIS area, for Target Stores, a division of the Dayton-Hudson Company.

Griffith was appointed instructor in computer science at Elizabethtown College in Pennsylvania, but the New York theatre was now only three hours away, allowing him to continue his interest in theatre and to take dance classes at the college and in New York. While at the college, he also came in contact with two nearby dinner theatres where he learned the business from the ground up, starting as an apprentice and leaving as a resident company manager.

After four years, Griffith left Elizabethtown College and went to New York, to pursue a serious interest in professional theatre. Griffith was hired in 1978 to assist in revitalizing a financially troubled dinner theatre in Ohio—the Carousel. His accomplishments at the Carousel include a complete financial turn-around of the corporation and its operations. On December 31, 1986, Griffith acquired 100 percent of the stock of the corporation and became sole owner. In 1988 the operation moved approximately 20 miles west to Akron, into a spectacular facility. Griffith spent over $1 million in remodeling and turned the Carousel into one of the most respected dinner theatres in the nation.

Castle Dinner Theatre
Gingerbread Castle Rd.
P.O. Box 69
Hamburg, NJ 07419

Opening date: 1989	Equity/non-Equity: non-Equity
Number on staff: 18–20	Ticket price range: $22.95–25.95
	Seating capacity: 150–200
Productions per year: 3–4	Average length of runs: 3–4 months
Buffet/table service: table	Stage type: full proscenium
Box office: (800) 626-6705	Owners: Brian Hammalton and Joe Difiglia

Locale: The Castle Dinner Theatre is nestled in the mountains of Sussex County, New Jersey. On the grounds of the historic Gingerbread Castle, the Castle Dinner Theatre has been a children's attraction since 1932. The building was built (in 1932) next to a charming babbling brook and includes three working fireplaces, wood-beamed cathedral ceilings, tiled floors, and little country shops (in the building).

History: In 1979 the entire complex was closed down, and it remained closed until it was purchased by Hammalton and Difiglia. Over $1 million in work and restoration went into the complex; it reopened in 1989, with an outside company producing the shows. After two years the owners felt that the theatre was not realizing its potential, so a completely new operations staff, production team, and marketing staff were brought in. Sales have been increasing steadily since the overhaul in management.

Staff: Brian Hammalton, Co-owner
        Joe Difiglia, Co-owner
        Scott Hart, Artistic Director
        Lynn Hart, Sales and Marketing
        Molly J. Earwood, Head Chef
        Wendy S. Meyer, Head Hostess
        Todd Difiglia, Stage Manager/Set Construction
        Don Schwenzer, Set Construction

Scott Hart has been involved in theatre for over 15 years. His credits include off Broadway, dinner theatre, summer stock, tours, and regional theatre, although his first love is dinner theatre. He was trained at the New York Academy of Theatrical Arts and his experience also includes several years in the special-effects industry for motion pictures.

Lynn Hart also has had a long career in theatre, including off Broadway, tours, summer stock, dinner theatre, and regional theatre. Her sales and marketing background comes from her training in the newspaper industry. Lynn is a certified teacher in the state of New Jersey and holds a masters degree in theatre from Montclair State College.

Comments: The Castle Dinner Theatre is proud to be one of the first dinner theatres in the state of New Jersey to offer a work study and apprentice program for students of theatre. The program runs from July through November and covers such topics as sales, costuming, lighting, set design and construction, and performing. Eight to ten positions are filled each season and applications are accepted.

Chanhassen Dinner Theatre
501 West 78th St.
P.O. Box 100
Chanhassen, MN 55317

Opening date: October 11, 1968

Number on staff: 260

Population of area (50 mi.): 2,250,000

Productions per year: 6–8

Buffet/table service: table

Box office: (612) 934-1525

Equity/non-Equity: Equity

Ticket price range: $14–43

Seating capacity: 572, 270, 190, and 125

Average length of runs: 17.5 weeks

Stage type: proscenium/thrust stages

Owner: International Broadcasting Corp.

Locale: Chanhassen Dinner Theatre is located 20 miles west of Minneapolis, Minnesota.

History: Chanhassen Dinner Theatre was founded and built by Herb and Carol Bloomberg in October of 1968. It was sold to International Broadcasting Corporation, owners of the Ice Capades and the Harlem Globetrotters, in June, 1989.

Staff: International Broadcasting Corp., Owner
    Jim Jude, President/CEO
    Michael Brindisi, Artistic Director
    Solveig Huseth, Company Manager
    George Topor, Food and Beverage Director
    David Shama, Marketing Director
    Kris Howland, Public Relations

Marlin Schoep, Comptroller
Pat Ahrens, Box Office Manager

Comments: Chanhassen Dinner Theatre opened its doors on October 11, 1968, with one 600-seat theatre, a restaurant, and a cocktail lounge. Founders Herbert and Carol Bloomberg put together their love of plays and their remarkable talents. Almost 25 years and 90,000 square feet later, they had created one of the nation's largest professional dinner theatre complexes, boasting four theatres under one roof.

Dedicated to artistic quality and a policy of performing full-length plays with complete costumes and sets, Chanhassen is one of the few theatres outside New York where guests can regularly enjoy big, professionally produced musicals.

Chanhassen is also the largest privately owned restaurant in Minnesota, typically serving over 1,000 dinners in the two-hour period before a production. *Gourmet* magazine declares Chanhassen to be "one of the very best" dinner theatres, and *Theatre Crafts* magazine calls it "the Cadillac of dinner theatres."

Circa '21 Dinner Playhouse
1828 3rd Ave.
Rock Island, IL 61201

Opening date: June 11, 1977

Number on staff: 70

Population of area (50 mi.): 625,000

Productions per year: 5–6

Buffet/table service: buffet

Box office: (309) 786-7733

Equity/non-Equity: non-Equity

Ticket price range: $20–23

Seating capacity: 336

Average length of runs: 8–12 weeks

Stage type: thrust/proscenium

Owners: Dinner Theatre Associates

Locale: Circa '21 is located at the Iowa-Illinois border, at the junction of I-80 and I-70, midway between Chicago and Des Moines.

History: The Circa '21 Dinner Playhouse is situated in a renovated 1920s vaudeville house and has produced national tours of *Pump Boys and Dinettes*, *Big River*, and *Oil City Symphony*. The theatre owns a costume rental business called The Show Business and is currently expanding into a commercial scene shop.

Staff: Dennis Hitchcock, Producer
Sherry Rhode-Heisel, General Manager
Sharon Cassidy, Business Manager
Thomas Beall, Production Manager/Designer
William Renk, Director of Audience Development

Comments: Besides a regular five-show season, Circa '21 also features celebrity attractions, a children's Christmas show, a Saturday family series, and the semi-regular Comedy Sporty, an improvisational comedy troupe.

Conklin Players Dinner Theatre
301 Conklin Ct.
P.O. Box 301
Goodfield, IL 61742

Opening date: October 31, 1975

Equity/non-Equity: non-Equity

Number on staff: 30

Ticket price range: $18.00–24.50

Population of area (50 mi.): 600,000

Seating capacity: 260

Productions per year: 6

Average length of runs: 10 weeks

Buffet/table service: buffet

Stage type: proscenium

Box office: (309) 965-2545

Owner: Chaunce Conklin

Locale: The theatre is in a rural setting off a major interstate highway midway between Peoria and Bloomington, in the heart of Illinois. Goodfield is also midway between Chicago and St. Louis. The Conklin Dinner Theatre's home is a former auction barn. The town of Eureka is seven miles to the north and houses the college that is Ronald Reagan's alma mater. Peoria is the home of the Caterpillar Tractor Company. The saying, "Will it play in Peoria?" still holds true as live theatre is abundant in the Peoria area, and Peorians can be a tough audience.

History: The Conklin Players Dinner Theatre has had the same ownership for 15 years. The former cattle-auction barn is part of an 1857 homestead and the brick home is now a bed-and-breakfast place. Guests can also take advantage of a dinner theatre/bed-and-breakfast package. The Conklin Players Dinner Theatre is the first and the oldest dinner theatre in central Illinois and also claims to have the longest-running melodrama in the state: *Love Rides the Rails.*

Staff: Chaunce Conklin, Producer/Director
Mary Simon, Business Manager/Costumer and Set Decorator
Tom Weber, Set Designer
Nick Firrantello, Stage Manager/Lighting
Jim Stout, Audio Operator
Amy Burgard, Props
Shirley Carroll, Box Office Manager/Group Reservations

Connecticut's Broadway Theatre
65 Tokeneke Rd.
Darien, CT 06820

Opening date: October 1977

Equity/non-Equity: Equity

Number on staff: 100

Ticket price range: $35–49

Population of area (50 mi.): 10 million

Seating capacity: 399

Productions per year: 4

Average length of runs: 8 weeks

Buffet/table service: table

Stage type: proscenium/thrust

Box office: (203) 655-7667   Operator: Jane Bergere, Executive
                                                           Producer

Locale: It is in affluent Fairfield County, Connecticut, approximately 40 miles north of Manhattan, off Route 95.

History: The theatre opened in October 1977. It was built and owned by John Grogan and Michael Minihan and a small group of investors. The opening show was *High Spirits*, directed by Morton DaCosta. The dinner theatre was taken over by new owners in 1984, with Jane Bergere at the helm. In 1990 the operation changed to table-service dining.

Staff: Jane Bergere, Chief Operating Officer/Executive Producer
        Fred Antidormi, Director of Food and Beverage
        Priscilla Squires, Director of Group Sales
        Gaelen Grogan, Box Office Manager
        Elaine Montello, Office Manager

Comments: With the theatre's close proximity to New York City, Broadway actors, directors, and designers are often used.

Cornwell's Dinner Theatre
18935 15½ Mile Rd.
P.O. Box 734
Marshall, MI 49068

Opening date: October 1987	Equity/non-Equity: non-Equity
Number on staff: 22	Ticket price range: $20.95–23.50
Population of area (50 mi.): 1.2 million plus	Seating capacity: 185
Productions per year: 5	Average length of runs: 9 weeks
Buffet/table service: combined	Stage type: proscenium
Box office: (616) 781-4315	Owner: David M. Pritchard

Locale: Cornwell's Dinner Theatre is located in an entertainment/gift shop/restaurant complex, three miles north of Marshall, called Turkeyville USA. Marshall is one of the nation's leading small cities, with over 100 designated historic sites. Its location in south central Michigan includes rolling farm land, with the major cities of Lansing, Jackson, Battle Creek, Kalamazoo, Ann Arbor, and Grand Rapids within a driving distance of one hour.

Staff: David M. Pritchard, Producer
        Dennis McKeen, Associate Producer
        Richard Gibson, Production Manager
        Julia Goodall, Operations Manager
        Kathy Kopolus, Group Sales
        Jody Anderson, Technical Director

Patti Cornwell, Audio Developer
Kathy LaPietra, Children's Theatre
Nancy Wade, House Manager
Shery Klienfelt, Bookkeeper

Comments: The main office of the theatre's operator, Pritchard Productions, Inc. (PPI) is also the office for the Michigan Theatre Association (MTA). PPI does the audition coordination for the MTA and the NDTA, in addition to coordinating the cross-promotions for the Great Lakes Theatre Conference members.

Country Dinner Playhouse
6875 S. Clinton
Englewood, CO 80112

Opening date: 1970	Equity/non-Equity: Equity
Number on staff: 55	Ticket price range: $17–23
Population of area (50 mi.): 1.5 million	Seating capacity: 470
Productions per year: 6	Average length of runs: 6–15 weeks
Buffet/table service: buffet	Stage type: round
Box office: (303) 799-1410	Owners: Sam Newton, Mary Boren

Staff: Sam Newton and Mary Boren, Owners
Sam Newton, General Manager
Bill McHale, Producer/Director
David Lovinggood, Manager
Joanie Buffington, Head Reservationist
Bob Buffington, House Manager

Derby Dinner Playhouse
525 Marriott Dr.
Clarksville, IN 47129

Opening date: November 1974	Equity/non-Equity: non-Equity
Number on staff: 12	Ticket price range: $11–21
Population of area (50 mi.): 967,500	Seating capacity: 568
Productions per year: varies	Average length of runs: 6–8 weeks
Buffet/table service: buffet	Stage type: arena-hydraulic lift
Box office: (812) 288-8281	Owners: Bekki Jo Schneider and
	Carolyn Lamb

Locale: The Derby's clientele attends from the bi-state urban area (Kentucky and Indiana). The only dinner theatre in a 200-mile radius, the Derby Dinner Playhouse is off all major interstates and provides free parking for all patrons.

Staff: Bekki Jo Schneider, Owner/Producer/Director
        Carolyn Lamb, Owner/General Manager
        Tom Thomas, House Manager
        Janette L. Hubert, Production Stage Manager
        Cynthia Lamb, Director of Marketing
        Phyllis Montgomery, Group Sales
        Betty Kelley, Box Office Manager
        Bob Lindsey, Night Manager
        Janet Davis, Administrative Assistant
        Daniel S. Mangan, Technical Director

Comments: The Derby Dinner Playhouse is now 18 years old and was originally part of a chain. Since it was purchased in 1984, the Derby has been a consistently viable business. Bekki Jo Schneider is a theatre professional and taught at two universities; helped develop the Arts in Education program for Kentucky; and is president of the National Dinner Theatre Association. Carolyn Lamb has been with the Derby since its inception and has led the organization to tight management and fiscal security. Carolyn has also served as the treasurer of the American Dinner Theatre Institute.

The Derby presents Broadway musicals, comedies, and mysteries. The theatre produces a new script nearly every year and the seasons also include some risk-taking productions, such as *Evita, Jesus Christ Superstar*, and *Born Yesterday*. A youth theatre and a season-ticket campaign are in operation.

Drury Lane Dinner Theatre
2500 W. 95th St.
Evergreen Park, IL 60642

Opening date: 1952	Equity/non-Equity: Equity
Number on staff: 32 plus	Ticket price range: $21.50–34.50
	Seating capacity: 821
Productions per year: 9	Average length of runs: 8–10 weeks
Buffet/table service: table	Stage type: arena
Box office: (708) 422-0404	Owner: John R. Lazzara

Locale: The theatre is on Chicago's near south side (15 minutes from the Loop), in the heart of the historical "Beverly Hills" area, one block from Western Avenue. There is easy access from Interstates 94, 294, 57, and 55, and from the Outer Drive. Free parking and valet service are offered.

History: The Drury Lane in Evergreen Park was the original Drury Lane built in Chicago by Anthony DeSantis in 1952.

Comments: The Drury Lane has four major productions each year: two musicals, one comedy, and one farce/mystery; also, three children's musicals, six star attractions, and three-to-six big-band-series productions. In the complex is the famed Martinique Restaurant and banquet facility featuring seven dining rooms, three bars, and a grand ballroom seating up to 1,000. The complex has been in operation for 40 years and a $1 million renovation has recently been completed.

Staff: John R. Lazzara, Executive Producer
        Raymond C. Lazzara, Assistant Producer
        Dr. James Lazzara, Financial Consultant
        Jon A. Putzke, Theatrical Manager
        Thomas Joyce, Production Manager
        John Minoque, Martinique General Manager
        Mary Gronek, Box Office Manager

Drury Lane Oakbrook Terrace Theatre
100 Drury Lane
Oakbrook Terrace, IL 60181

Opening date: October 1984	Equity/non-Equity: Equity
	Ticket price range: $17.00–37.75
Population of area (50 mi.): 8 million	Seating capacity: 971
Productions per year: 5–6	Average length of runs: 8–10 weeks
Buffet/table service: table/Sunday brunch	Stage type: proscenium
Box office: (708) 530-8300	Owner: Anthony DeSantis

Locale: Located 30 minutes west of downtown Chicago and 20 minutes south of O'Hare Airport, the Drury Lane Oakbrook Terrace Theatre is situated in a community housing headquarters for many major corporations.

History: Anthony DeSantis opened his first Drury Lane in 1952, and it is still located in Evergreen Park. The Drury Lane Oakbrook Terrace is the fifth Drury Lane, and the only one still owned by DeSantis.

Staff: Anthony DeSantis, Owner
        Diane Van Lente, President/Managing Director
        Travis Stockley, Artistic Director

Dutch Apple Dinner Theatre
510 Centerville Rd.
Lancaster, PA 17601

Opening date: April 3, 1987	Equity/non-Equity: non-Equity
Number on staff: 100	Ticket price range: $14–27
Population of area (50 mi.): 3 million	Seating capacity: 350

Productions per year: 7

Average length of runs: 8–10 weeks

Buffet/table service: buffet

Stage type: proscenium

Box office: (717) 898-1900

Owners: Thomas and Deborah Prather

Locale: Lancaster County, Pennsylvania, is the heart of Pennsylvania's Amish farmland—one of the top tourist destinations in the East. It is also a solid financial base of agriculture and industrial development.

Staff: Deborah Prather, Executive Producer/Owner
        Thomas Prather, Artistic Director/Owner
        Joe Mackin, Business Manager
        Denise Simpson, Marketing Director
        Joan Payne, Group Sales Director

Tom and Deborah Prather have presented professional theatre in Pennsylvania since 1964 and have established themselves and produced plays in 13 different cities. Tom Prather is a past president of the National Dinner Theatre Association.

Fanny Hill Inn & Dinner Theatre
3919 Crescent Ave.
Eau Claire, WI 54703

Opening date: September 1978

Equity/non-Equity: non-Equity

Number on staff: 4

Ticket price range: $21.95–24.95

Population of area (50 mi.): 100,000

Seating capacity: 190

Productions per year: 5

Average length of runs: 8–10 weeks

Buffet/table service: table

Stage type: proscenium

Box office: (715) 836-8184

Owner: Fanny Hill Ltd.

Staff: Fanny Hill Ltd., Owner
        Larry Barr, President
        Don Hodgins, Director
        Lois Hodgins, Group Sales Manager
        Scott Rayburn, Stage Manager
        Mark Kulas, Master Carpenter

Garbeau's Dinner Theatre
12401 Folsom Blvd.
Rancho Cordova, CA 95742-6413

Opening date: October 1981

Equity/non-Equity: non-Equity

Number on staff: 40–50

Ticket price range: $20–27

Population of area (50 mi.): 1.1 million   Seating capacity: 225
Productions per year: 6   Average length of runs: 8–9 weeks
Buffet/table service: table   Stage type: modified thrust
Box office: (916) 985-6361   Owner: Bo Butkovich

Locale: The theatre is located in the historic Nimbus Winery building, Highway 50 at Hazel Avenue, in Rancho Cordova, about 15 miles east of Sacramento.

History: Garbeau's opened in 1981 in a renovated pizza parlor in Sacramento with 115 seats. The theatre moved to its present location in 1984 and added over 100 seats.

Staff: Bo Butkovich, Producer/Owner
        Diane Hofsommer, Managing Director
        John Higgins, Artistic Director
        John Beaushausen, General Manager
        Tim Anderson, Technical Director/Scenic Designer
        Sunan Logan, Executive Chef
        Enid Baldcock, Assistant Manager
        Michael Baldasarra, Box Office Manager

Genetti Dinner Theatre
Route 309
Hazleton, PA 18201

Opening date: New facility, 1991   Equity/non-Equity: non-Equity
Number on staff: 20   Ticket price range: $21–27
Population of area (50 mi.): 500,000   Seating capacity: 350
Productions per year: 7   Average length of runs: 5–6 weeks
Buffet/table service: both   Stage type: thrust
Box office: (717) 455-3691   Owner: Best Western Genetti Motor
                                                  Lodge

Locale: Hazleton's immediate area has a population of 50,000 (average age is higher than the state average), and the theatre is located in northern Pennsylvania at the intersection of I-80 and I-81. The business base is provided by diversified light industry. Hazleton is located 25 miles south of the Wilkes-Barre/Scranton area and 45 miles north of Allentown and Bethlehem.

History: Genetti's was opened in 1975, with 275 seats and a proscenium stage, as part of the Best Western Genetti Motor Lodge and Restaurant complex. On August 30, 1989, a major fire destroyed the dinner theatre building. In 1991 a new 350-seat dinner theatre opened, with a thrust stage.

Staff: Bill Genetti, Producer

Comments: Previous producers for Genetti's have included Tom Prather, owner of the Dutch Apple Dinner Theatre, and Richard Akins, owner of the Jupiter Dinner Theatre.

Golden Apple Dinner Theatre
25 N. Pineapple Ave.
Sarasota, FL 34236

Opening date: December 11, 1971   Equity/non-Equity: Equity

Number on staff: 15 plus   Ticket price range: $19.50–26.00

Population of area (50 mi.): 225,000   Seating capacity: 279

Productions per year: 8–9   Average length of runs: 6–8 weeks

Buffet/table service: buffet   Stage type: 3/4 thrust

Box office: (813) 366-5454   Owner: Robert E. Turoff

Locale: The Golden Apple is located in a resort and cultural community 60 miles south of the Tampa/St. Petersburg area. Sarasota has many fine attractions, including the home of the Ringling Museum, the Asolo State Theatre, the Chicago White Sox spring training camp, white sand beaches, exclusive shopping, and the Golden Apple Dinner Theatre.

History: The Golden Apple was originally opened in 1971, with a second Golden Apple opening in St. Petersburg in 1981. The third was opened in Venice, Florida, in 1989.

Staff: Robert E. Turoff, Executive Director/Producer
          Roberta M. Turoff, Associate Producer
          Felicia Antolik, Business Manager
          Lyla FitzGerald, Production Coordinator
          William Sherry, Stage Manager/Technical Director
          B. G. FitzGerald, Costumer
          Tom Dillickraeth, Theatre Manager

Comments: Over 200 productions have been staged at the Sarasota Golden Apple, along with five world premieres of original productions, and these have won numerous design awards.

Ingersoll Dinner Theatre
3711 Ingersoll Ave.
Des Moines, IA 50312

Opening date: 1976   Equity/non-Equity: non-Equity
                                                                    Ticket price range: $20.00–27.50

Population of area (50 mi.): 500,000 plus   Seating capacity: 275

Productions per year: 9–10   Average length of runs: 5–7 weeks
Buffet/table service: buffet   Stage type: proscenium thrust
Box office: (515) 274-4686   Owner: Charles Carnes

Locale: Located at the junction of Interstates 80 and 35, the Ingersoll has become an ideal attraction for groups. It is also the only continuously operating dinner theatre in Iowa.

History: The Ingersoll Dinner Theatre has been run by Charles Carnes since its opening in 1976. It has expanded to the point of presenting guest artists and children's theatre productions in addition to Broadway musicals and comedies.

Staff: Charles Carnes, Producer/Owner
        D. J. Horrigan, Artistic Director
        Charmin Sterbenz, Director of Marketing and Communications
        Barb Merrill, Group Sales Director
        Bart Herman, Box Office Manager
        Chris Behle, Evening Manager
        David Barr, Technical Director

Comments: The Ingersoll was the first to present children's theatre productions in central Iowa. The Ingersoll won an award from the Iowa Broadcasters' Association in the television-commercial category in 1992. Carnes has been the secretary for the National Dinner Theatre Association for over three years.

Jupiter Theatre
1001 East Indiantown Rd.
Jupiter, FL 33477

Opening date: November 14, 1989   Equity/non-Equity: Equity
Number on staff: 49   Ticket price range: $38.50–47.50
                                          Seating capacity: 428
Productions per year: 9–10   Average length of runs: 5 weeks
Buffet/table service: table   Stage type: proscenium
Box office: (407) 746-5566   Owner: Richard C. Akins

Locale: Jupiter, Florida, is an attractive, affluent community located 20 minutes north of Palm Beach, in Palm Beach County, on the Atlantic Ocean.

History: The Jupiter Theatre was built in 1979 by the actor Burt Reynolds and was sold in 1989 to a producer, Richard C. Akins.

Staff: Richard C. Akins, Owner
        Paulette Winn, General Manager
        Brian Cronin, Associate Producer
        Cherie Panian, Comptroller

Bruce Fellman, Sales Manager
Avery Schreiber, Artistic Director
Pamela Smith, Public Relations Director
Janina Akins, Creative Director

La Comedia Restaurant and Theater
765 W. Central Ave.
P.O. Box 204
Springboro, OH 45066

Opening date: 1979	Equity/non-Equity: non-Equity
Number on staff: 100+	Ticket price range: $23.95–31.95
Population of area (50 mi.): 3 million plus	Seating capacity: 618
Productions per year: 5 plus	Average length of runs: 8–12 weeks
Buffet/table service: buffet	Stage type: thrust
Box office: (513) 228-9333	Owner: Kim Klopcic

Locale: Located between two major metropolitan areas, Dayton and Cincinnati, Ohio, La Comedia is easily accessible by Interstate 75.

History: The Klopcic family purchased La Comedia in 1988, and the president, Kim Klopcic, has enhanced the food service operation with his considerable restaurant background.

Staff: Kim Klopcic, Owner
        Bob Stahl, Vice President
        John J. Turchon, Director of Sales
        Marie Leiding, Director of Group Sales

Comments: In addition to the regular performance schedule, special concerts and shows are presented. La Comedia is available for special uses and meetings as well.

Lake George Dinner Theatre
Holiday Inn, Canada St.
P.O. Box 4623
Lake George, NY 12804

Opening date: 1967	Equity/non-Equity: Equity
Number on staff: 2	Ticket price range: $20–39
	Seating capacity: 175
Productions per year: 1	Average length of runs: 18 weeks
Buffet/table service: table	Stage type: flexible
Box office: (518) 668-5781	Owner: David P. Eastwood

Locale: The theatre is located in a small resort town about four hours north of New York City. The basic attraction of the area is the beautiful surrounding landscape. The Lake George Dinner Theatre is the only professional theatre within a 60-mile radius and provides a valuable mainstay attraction. Audiences are comprised of 60 percent groups, 35 percent individuals, and 5 percent show-only patrons.

History: The dinner theatre was originated by David Eastwood as a non-professional summer stock in Lake George. In 1975 it moved to the local Holiday Inn, became an Equity-affiliated dinner theatre; it has remained there even though the ownership of the hotel has changed hands.

Staff: David P. Eastwood, Owner/Operator
        Sharon Reynolds, General Manager

Comments: In 1979 the murder mystery comedy called *Shear Madness* played in Lake George and was such a huge success that it was brought back in 1980. Producer David Eastwood and the director, Bruce Jordan, then obtained the play from its author, Paul Portner, and revised it; it played in Boston in 1980, where it became the longest-running play in American theatre history. It has played in other cities across the United States.

Lawrence Welk Resort Theatre
8860 Lawrence Welk Dr.
Escondido, CA 92026

Opening date: 1981	Equity/non-Equity: Equity
Number on staff: 25	Ticket price range: $26–39
Population of area (50 mi.): 3 million	Seating capacity: 331
Productions per year: 6	Average length of runs: 9 weeks
Buffet/table service: buffet	Stage type: proscenium
Box office: (619) 749-3448	Owner: Welk Group, Inc.

Locale: The theatre is part of the Lawrence Welk Resort, which is located in a picturesque valley eight miles north of Escondido, California. The resort has three golf courses, tennis, swimming, a hotel, a restaurant, time-share condominiums, and a commercial center made up of retail gift shops, a market, and a delicatessen.

History: The late Lawrence Welk purchased the resort in 1964 and the Welk Group, Inc., still owns and operates the property. The theatre opened in 1981 as part of the Lawrence Welk Museum (the theatre lobby). The resort has expanded to 1,000 acres since Welk's original purchase in 1964.

Staff: H. M. DeSantis, General Manager/Vice President/Executive Producer
        Jackie Nelson, Assistant to General Manager/Vice President/Executive
          Producer

Frank Wayne, Artistic Director
Larry Cady, Theatre Administrator
Sean Coogan, Box Office Manager

Marriott's Lincolnshire Theatre
10 Marriott Dr.
Lincolnshire, IL 60069

Opening date: 1977	Equity/non-Equity: Equity
Number on staff: 50	Ticket price range: $30
Population of area (50 mi.): 5 million	Seating capacity: 862
Productions per year: 5	Average length of runs: 10–12 weeks
Buffet/table service: table	Stage type: arena
Box office: (708) 634-0200	Owner/Operator: Marriott Corp.

Locale: Located in the Marriott's Lincolnshire Resort complex, the award-winning Lincolnshire Theatre features an 870-seat arena stage with excellent sight lines and amplification. It's just steps away from the complete entertainment facilities of the resort.

History: Marriott's Lincolnshire Theatre opened in conjunction with Marriott's Lincolnshire Resort, under the name Drury Lane Theatre North, presenting well-known stars in proven comedies and light drama. In 1977 the theatre assumed its current name and converted fully to a musical theatre in 1979, producing classics, premieres of new works, and seldom-seen works. The theatre has garnered numerous Jefferson Awards and nominations from 1982. Its list of world premieres includes *Give My Regards to Broadway*, *Star Time*, *Matador*, *History Loves Company*, and *Annie Warbucks*.

Staff: Kary M. Walker, Executive Producer
Dyanne Earley, Artistic Director
Lauren Johnson, Director of Marketing
Terry James, Director of Public Relations/Advertising
Barbara Kavanagh, Box Office Manager
Brigid Brown, Production Manager

Kary M. Walker has served as producer for Marriott's Lincolnshire Theatre since 1979, presenting more than 50 productions that have been nominated, in various categories, for more than 100 Joseph Jefferson Awards. Walker is from Conroe, Texas, and is a Vietnam veteran. He is an original member of the National Alliance of Musical Theatre Producers, serves on the board of the Apple Tree Theater, is on the Advisory Board of the Actors' Equity program "Season of Concern: The Theatre Community Fights AIDS," and is second vice president of the American Dinner Theatre Institute.

Dyanne Earley received a Jefferson Award nomination as director, for her work on *My Fair Lady*, and has also directed Marriott's productions of *Oliver!*, *Camelot, Cabaret, 70 Girls 70*, and *Pump Boys and Dinettes*, in addition to several of the Lincolnshire's Theatre for Young Audiences productions.

Murry's Dinner Playhouse
6323 Asher Ave.
K-Mart Shopping Center
Little Rock, AR 72204

Opening date: June 6, 1967

Number on staff: 44

Population of area (50 mi.): 750,000

Productions per year: 10

Buffet/table service: buffet

Box office: (501) 562-3131

Equity/non-Equity: non-Equity

Ticket price range: $17–21

Seating capacity: 304

Average length of runs: 4–7 weeks

Stage type: proscenium

Owner: Ginger McEntire

History: Murry's won the 1989 Diner's Award for Best Live Entertainment, presented by the *Arkansas Gazette*.

Staff: Ike Murry McEntire, President/General Manager
Ginger McEntire, Secretary/Treasurer
Lawanna Hardin, Office Manager
Joan Brown, Group Sales
Laura Yielding, Group Sales
Glenn Gilbert, Director
Russ Talley, Stage Manager
Denzil Roland, Chef

Naples Dinner Theatre
1025 Piper Blvd.
Naples, FL 33942

Opening date: October 1975

Number on staff: 35

Population of area (50 mi.): 500,000

Productions per year: 9

Buffet/table service: buffet

Box office: (813) 597-6031

Equity/non-Equity: non-Equity

Ticket price range: $24–35

Seating capacity: 349

Average length of runs: 4–7 weeks

Stage type: thrust

Owner: Julius Fisk, General Partner

Locale: Naples is a modern community with all services available. Naples is very tourist oriented and boasts a very pleasant climate.

Staff: Julius Fisk, General Partner
Jim Fargo, Reservations Director

Paul Fiske, General Manager
Phillipe La Croix, Master Chef
Sandi Amarol, Director of Marketing
Angel Cavill, Group Sales Director
Andrew J. Poleszak, Costume Designer
David Kemp, Technical Director
Donald Rupp, Stage Manager

Jim Fargo has been in the dinner theatre business as an actor, director, and producer for over 20 years. He has directed over 200 productions throughout the country. Andrew J. Poleszak is a graduate of the State University of New York at Buffalo, with a degree in art education. He has designed over 50 shows, winning rave reviews from the public as well as critics.

Comments: Naples Dinner Theatre facilities include a carpentry shop, costume shop, rehearsal hall, and housing facilities for actors.

Omni Dinner Theatre
777 Waterside Dr.
Norfolk, VA 23510

Opening date: October 1986	Equity/non-Equity: non-Equity
Number on staff: 17	Ticket price range: $18.95–21.95
Population of area (50 mi.): 1 million	Seating capacity: 150
Productions per year: 8	Average length of runs: 6–8 weeks
Buffet/table service: table	Stage type: arena
Box office: (804) 627-7773	Owner: Omni International Hotels

Locale: The Omni Dinner Theatre is located in the Omni Norfolk Hotel, just off the main lobby. The dinner theatre and hotel cater to an area including Norfolk, Virginia Beach, Hampton, Newport News, Chesapeake, and Suffolk. The area also contains the largest naval port in the country, consequently serving a large number of military personnel.

Staff: Wanda McAllister, Manager
        Maxine Boyd, Reservationist

Comments: All productions at the Omni are handled by Lime-Light Productions, Inc. The Omni Dinner Theatre has been under the ownership of the Omni Hotel since its inception.

Oregon Ridge Dinner Theatre
13403 Beaver Dam Rd.
Cockeysville, MD 21030

Opening date: April 9, 1983

Number on staff: 3–5

Productions per year: 3–4

Buffet/table service: buffet

Box office: (410) 771-8427

Equity/non-Equity: non-Equity

Ticket price range: $19.00–28.50

Seating capacity: 175

Average length of runs: 3 months plus

Stage type: round and 3/4

Owner: Baltimore Actors' Theatre, Inc.

Locale: The Oregon Ridge Dinner Theatre is beautifully located near the Marriott Hunt Valley Inn, the Embassy Suites, Holiday Inn, Hampton Inn, and the Hunt Valley Mall. It is about 20 minutes from Baltimore's Inner Harbor and a one-hour drive from Washington, D.C. Its charming country setting makes it ideal for an overnight excursion.

History: This dinner theatre is a unique operation run by a non-profit organization in association with the Baltimore County Recreation and Parks Department. The facility was totally renovated by the Baltimore Actors' Theatre, Inc., and functions both as a children's theatre and an adult musical theatre. It also showcases performances by members of the Baltimore Actors' Theatre Conservatory, a fully accredited college preparatory school of the arts for grades 1–12. The theatre's food service is catered since it has no kitchen facilities.

Staff: Patricia Gresser, General Manager

Riverfront Dinner Theatre
Delaware River, at Poplar St.
Philadelphia, PA 19123

Opening date: 1975

Number on staff: 75

Population of area (50 mi.): 4 million

Productions per year: 5

Buffet/table service: buffet

Box office: (215) 925-7000

Equity/non-Equity: non-Equity

Ticket price range: $20.95–32.95

Seating capacity: 400–500

Average length of runs: 10 weeks

Owner: Robert Tabas, Executive Director

Locale: Sitting on the longest pier on the Delaware River, the Riverfront Dinner Theatre provides stunning views of the river traffic and the Ben Franklin Bridge. It is only five minutes from all center-city hotels and is part of the Riverfront complex that includes a jazz club and banquet facility.

Staff: Robert Tabas, Owner/Executive Director
       Robert Prince, General Manager

Roger Rocka's Music Hall
1226 N. Wishon Ave.
Fresno, CA 93728

Opening date: 1978

Number on staff: 41 plus

Population (local): 350,000

Productions per year: 6

Buffet/table service: both

Box office: (209) 266-9494

Equity/non-Equity: non-Equity

Ticket price range: $14.00–26.50

Seating capacity: 252

Average length of runs: 7–10 weeks

Stage type: proscenium/thrust

Owner: Roger Rocka

Locale: Roger Rocka's Music Hall is located in the Tower District of Fresno and, since the theatre's founding in 1978, restaurants and shops have blossomed in this older neighborhood, making it something of an arty, quaint community center.

History: Roger Rocka's Music Hall is different in structure than most dinner theatres. The restaurant and bar operations are owned and operated by Rocka, a former television news anchor. The entertainment is provided by a production organization called the Good Company Players, which has a full-time staff of 11. The performers are members of the local community and are volunteers. The Good Company Players started as a summer musical theatre group composed of current and former students and faculty of the local State University. Since 1978, Good Players has evolved into a year-round production company.

Staff: Roger Rocka, Owner/Operator
       Dan Pessano, Managing Director, Good Company Players

Comments: The Music Hall currently maintains approximately 3,400 season ticket holders. Another 20–25 percent of the patrons are from tour groups. The balance of the seats are sold to local single-ticket buyers.

Royal Palm Dinner Theatre
303 Golfview Dr.
Boca Raton, FL 33432

Opening date: December 1979

Productions per year: 6

Buffet/table service: table

Box office: (407) 392-3755

Equity/non-Equity: Equity

Ticket price range: $31–34

Seating capacity: 270

Average length of runs: 2–3 months

Stage type: arena

Owner: Jan McArt

Locale: The Royal Palm is situated in the plush community of Boca Raton and the theatre is located in one of the most beautiful shopping plazas in the country.

History: In December 1977, a "crown jewel" was created in the Pink Plaza in Boca Raton, Florida—the Royal Palm Dinner Theatre. Because Jan McArt wanted to spend more time with her mother, who lived in Boca, and because Jan was amazed that there was no professional theatre at that time in the area, she began to work on a dream that she shared with her friend and business partner, Bill Orhelein: to have a theatre of their own.

The food originally was buffet style, although many critics said it was the best buffet in town. Opting for a more elegant atmosphere, the menu was changed to table service with gourmet dishes. Although Jan lost valuable help, support, and advice when her partner, Bill Orhelein, died in 1987, she continued with their dream. Jan McArt's Cabaret Theatre in Key West was opened; a world premiere occurred in Coral Springs, Florida; she began the Library Theatre in Fort Lauderdale, and Jan McArt's International Room at the Marco Polo Hotel in Miami Beach; and she opened *The Prince of Central Park* before sending it to Broadway.

Jan McArt, singer, actress, theatre producer and owner, was once proclaimed by the London *Star* as "one of the most beautiful and talented women in the world." Arturo Toscanini, after seeing her as Musetta in NBC-TV's production of *La Boheme*, exclaimed: "Miss McArt's Musetta is the finest I have ever seen or heard." The critics shared the maestro's point of view and she was nominated to receive an Emmy. McArt has toured throughout the world and appeared in a plethora of shows, including the world premiere of Mike Todd's musical, *Around the World in 80 Days*. McArt has appeared on nationally televised shows and in her own supper-club act at the Hotel Pierre in New York, the famed St. Regis, the Coconut Grove in Los Angeles, the Blackstone and the Drake in Chicago, and the Society and the Colony in London. McArt starred in *Sweet Bird of Youth* at the Ruth Foreman Theatre in Miami and won the Carbonell Award as Best Actress in a Musical, for her portrayal of Kay Goodman in *Nite Club Confidential* in 1985. Aside from her acting career, Jan is a founder and owner of the Royal Palm Dinner Theatre, and of Jan McArt's Room at the Marco Polo Hotel in Miami Beach.

Shawnee Playhouse
River Rd.
P.O. Box 159
Shawnee-on-Delaware, PA 18356

	Equity/non-Equity: non-Equity
	Ticket price range: $14–19
Population of area (50 mi.): 250,000	Seating capacity: 220
Productions per year: 5	Average length of runs: 5 weeks

Buffet/table service: buffet   Stage type: proscenium

Box office: (717) 421-5093   Owner: Charles Kirkwood

Locale: The Shawnee Playhouse is in the heart of the Pocono Mountains and part of the resort, the Shawnee Group, just off I-80 near the Delaware Water Gap.

History: In the late 1940s and early 1950s, the Shawnee Playhouse was the home of the "Fred Waring and the Pennsylvanians" radio hour. The facility was torched by an arsonist in 1985 and was rebuilt and improved in 1987.

Staff: Charles Kirkwood, Owner
        Scott K. Douglas, General Manager
        Noreen Manda, Marketing Director

Comments: The Shawnee Playhouse does its casting in New York City (non-Equity) and the cast sizes range from 12 to 20 performers. The technical staff (technical directors, stage managers, costumers, set designers, and lighting designers) is also hired in New York, or from among applicants from graduate schools and from resumes. The Shawnee Playhouse was awarded the Pennsylvania State Commerce Department Phoenix Award for cultural enhancement.

Showboat Dinner Theatre
3405 Ulmerton Rd.
Clearwater, FL 34622

Productions per year: 8   Seating capacity: 428

Buffet/table service: buffet   Average length of runs: 6 weeks

Box office: (813) 573-3777   Stage type: proscenium

Equity/non-Equity: Equity   Owner: Virginia L. Sherwood

Ticket price range: $21.40–$28.90

Locale: The Showboat, originally built by Dow Sherwood, is located in Clearwater, Florida, south of Tampa/St. Pete on Florida's beautiful Gulf Coast.

Staff: Virginia Sherwood, Owner/Executive Producer
        Stanley Ziemba, Vice President
        Cathy Waldauer, Group Sales

The Stage Door Theatre (Conley's)
Route 30
Irwin, PA 15642

Opening date: 1976   Equity/non-Equity: non-Equity

Number on staff: 15   Ticket price range: $18–28

Population of area (50 mi.): 2 million   Seating capacity: 250

Productions per year: 9   Average length of runs: 2 months

Buffet/table service: combined

Box office: (800) 766-7824   Owners: Conley Family

Locale: The Stage Door Theatre is located within Conley's Motor Lodge on U.S. Route 30, one mile west of the Pennsylvania Turnpike, exit 7.

Staff: James Conley, Operator
        Tim Brady, Director
        Mindy Ross-Stabler, Choreographer
        Ron Gatty, Emcee
        Denny Doran, Music Director

Tim Brady, now in his tenth season at Conley's as a performer, has been their director since 1986 and the co-writer of all productions. Brady has performed in a variety of Broadway-type musicals, has appeared with the Civic Light Opera Company, and can be seen in the movie *Silence of the Lambs*, with Jodi Foster.

Sunshine Dinner Playhouse
115 West Kirby
Champaign, IL 61820

Opening date: July 5, 1980	Equity/non-Equity: non-Equity
Number on staff: 6	Ticket price range: $16–20
Population of area (50 mi.): 350,000	Seating capacity: 200
Productions per year: 5–6	Average length of runs: 9 weeks
Buffet/table service: both	Stage type: thrust
Box office: (217) 359-4503	Owner: Arthur L. Barnes

Locale: Sunshine Dinner Playhouse is located two-and-a-half hours south of Chicago and two hours west of Indianapolis. Champaign, Illinois, primarily a farming area, is the home of the University of Illinois.

History: The theatre originally opened on July 5, 1980, and changed ownership in February 1988.

Staff: Arthur L. Barnes, Owner
        Jerry Gulledge, Associate Producer/Children's Theatre
        Rozita Wade, Office Manager
        Andrew Lund, Group Sales
        Susan McMahon, Reservations Director

Sylvia's Class Act
5115 N.E. Sandy Blvd.
Portland, OR 97213

Opening date: September 1985

Number on staff: 2

Equity/non-Equity: non-Equity

Ticket price range: $18.95–22.95

Seating capacity: 90

Productions per year: 4–5

Average length of runs: 10 weeks

Buffet/table service: table

Stage type: proscenium

Box office: (503) 281-0411

Owners: Patti Gosser and Roberta Barger

Located on N.E. Sandy Boulevard in what's known as Upper Hollywood, Sylvia's Class Act is approximately 15 minutes from the Portland International Airport.

History: Sylvia's opened in September 1985. Theatre had been a longtime passion of Sylvia, and, by opening her own dinner theatre, she saw her dream come to fruition. Sylvia's Class Act is indeed Portland's first dinner theatre. It was also the first theatre to produce *Nunsense* in the Portland area. Sylvia sold the restaurant and theatre to her two daughters, Patti and Roberta, in October 1988; her dream lives on through her daughters.

Staff: Patti Gosser, Owner
        Roberta Barger, Owner/Vice President
        LeeAnn Loveland, Manager

Toby's Dinner Theatre
South Enhance Rd.
Box 1003
Columbia, MD 21044

Opening date: December 3, 1979

Equity/non-Equity: non-Equity

Ticket price range: $25.10–29.35

Population of area (50 mi.): 1 million

Seating capacity: 300

Productions per year: 4

Average length of runs: 15 weeks

Buffet/table service: buffet

Stage type: arena

Box office: (301) 730-8311

Owner/operator: Toby Orenstein

Locale: Toby's Dinner Theatre, formerly the Garland Dinner Theatre, is located midway between Baltimore and Washington, D.C.

Staff: Toby Orenstein, Owner
        Hal Orenstein, Owner
        Steve Lewis, Owner

David Schaffer, General Manager
Tony Toffon, Manager
Jean Kain, Group Sales Manager
Bob Moore, Kitchen Manager
Vicki Johnson, Production Manager

Toby Orenstein is the owner and artistic director of the operation. She directs all musical productions. Toby, also an educator, taught at Catholic University and has her own theatre school in Columbia. She was awarded the title of Woman of the Year in 1987 and was recently named Outstanding Artist of the Year. Toby dedicates herself to presenting a wide variety of musicals and her theatre is often called "the theatre to dare," due to the show selections she has produced, some of which include *Sweeney Todd*, *Baby*, and *Into the Woods*.

Towsontowne Dinner Theatre
7800 York Rd.
Towson, MD 21204

Opening date: 1982	Equity/non-Equity: non-Equity
Number on staff: 10	Ticket price range: $25.95
	Seating capacity: 250
Productions per year: 5	Average length of runs: 10 weeks
Buffet/table service: buffet	Stage type: proscenium thrust
Box office: (410) 321-6595	Owner: F. Scott Black

Locale: The theatre is located in the heart of Towson, next to Towson State University, 15 minutes from the Inner Harbor of Baltimore.

Staff: F. Scott Black, Owner/Operator/Artistic Director
        Diane Trowbridge, General Manager
        James Hunnicutt, Director of Sales

West End Dinner Theatre
4615 Duke St.
Alexandria, VA 22304

Opening date: February 29, 1984	Equity/non-Equity: non-Equity; letters of agreement
Number on staff: 85	Ticket price range: $21–33
Population of area (50 mi.): 4 million plus	Seating capacity: 350
Productions per year: 4–5	Average length of runs: 3 months
Buffet/table service: table	Stage type: proscenium
Box office: (703) 370-2500	Owner: James J. Matthews

Locale: The West End Dinner Theatre is located in a heavily populated metropolitan area, only five minutes from Old Town, Alexandria, Virginia, and minutes
from the monuments in downtown Washington, D.C. Its location is convenient
to many East Coast landmarks, such as Annapolis, Baltimore, Manassas, and
Fredericksburg.

History: The theatre opened February 29, 1984. Originally begun as an Equity
theatre, the West End was then changed into a non-Equity house. Several
guest-artist contracts (letters of agreement with Equity) are arranged each year.
There are also Children's Theatre productions offered on Saturday afternoons.
The operation has expanded to include concerts, special events, catering, politi-
cal/social fund raisers, wedding receptions, and awards banquets. All aspects of
the operation are completely run in-house, from the food preparation and service
to production design and execution of props, set design, costume building/design,
and sound design. In 1989, the West End Dinner Theatre won the Alex Award,
which is given by the Alexandria Chamber of Commerce in recognition of
contributions to the theatrical community.

Staff: James J. Matthews, Owner
        Robert J. Test, Producer
        Kevin J. Sheehan, General Manager
        Brendan J. Sheehan, House Manager
        Lisa Renee Vespia, House Manager
        Tracy Burling, Group Sales Director
        Geoffrey Eichhorn, Special Events Coordinator
        Elaine M. Randolph, Production Stage Manager
        Spencer Barrett, Technical Director/Set Designer

Westchester Broadway Theatre
1 Broadway Plaza
Elmsford, NY 10523

Opening date: new facility, February 13, 1991 Equity/non-Equity: Equity
Operation opening: July 9, 1974
Number on staff: 140   Ticket price range: $32–50
Population of area (50 mi.): 9 million   Seating capacity: 449
Productions per year: 3–4   Average length of runs:
                                                  15–20 weeks
Buffet/table service: table   Stage type: thrust
Box office: (914) 592-2222   Owners: William B. Stutler and
                                                  Robert J. Funking

Locale: The Westchester Broadway Theatre (formerly An Evening Dinner Theatre) is in the heart of Westchester County, approximately 20 miles north of

Manhattan, four miles west of White Plains. Westchester County has a diversified population that in some ways can be considered an extension of New York City.

Staff: William B. Stutler, Owner/Producer
        Robert J. Funking, Owner/Producer
        David Cunningham, Associate Producer
        Lisa Tiso, Associate Producer
        Allan Gruet, Public and Press Relations
        Antonio Dinis, Executive Chef
        Kathleen Conroy, Group Sales Manager
        Liz Conciatori, Box Office Manager
        Leslie Davis, Advertising Director

As the longest-running, 52-weeks-a-year Equity theatre in New York State, the Westchester Broadway's Bill Stutler and Bob Funking have produced more shows than have most established Broadway producers. Having created An Evening Dinner Theatre from the ground up in 1974 and changing to a newly built facility in 1991, the producers have established the theatre as a cultural mainstay in Westchester County. Prior to moving to the new location, An Evening Dinner Theatre had served over 2 million customers, produced 82 Broadway productions, hosted over 5,000 groups, aided the fund-raising efforts of over 5,000 charitable organizations, and provided employment for over 2,158 professional actors and musicians.

Zellmer's Main Street Dinner Theatre
45 N. Main St.
Farmington, IL 61531

Opening date: November 1988	Equity/non-Equity: non-Equity
Number on staff: 25	Ticket price range: $18–21
Population of area (50 mi.): 250,000	Seating capacity: 140
Productions per year: 5	Average length of runs: 2–3 months
Buffet/table service: buffet	Stage type: proscenium
Box office: (309) 245-4415	Owner: Don Grant Zellmer

Locale: Zellmer's Main Street Dinner Theatre is located 25 minutes west of Peoria, in the heart of scenic Spoon River country, in a small rural farm community.

History: Zellmer's Main Street Dinner Theatre is an intimate, warm, and inviting theatre situated in a former silent-movie house built in 1917. The structure was also home to touring Vaudeville acts, and it enjoys a rich tradition of entertainment. Now renovated and operated as a dinner theatre, it comfortably seats guests on four levels, allowing excellent sight lines to the stage from any point in the theatre.

Staff: Don Grant Zellmer, Owner/Director
        Di-Anne Harper Zellmer, Assistant Manager
        Ron Kimbrell, Assistant Manager/New Projects Developer
        Marquita Jean Welch, Group Sales Director/Technical Director
        Marianne Campbell, Business Manager

Don Grant Zellmer previously owned and managed Peoria's Cabaret Music Theatre. Before coming to Peoria in 1984, Zellmer worked in community, summer-stock, and dinner theatres, and on film and television. He also appeared in the move *Creator*, with Peter O'Toole. For several years Zellmer travelled with Cargill Theatrical Productions as a director/choreographer and featured artist. He also toured with nightclub acts and show groups, opening for such acts as Dionne Warwick and the Spinners.

   Di-Anne Harper Zellmer began her professional performing career in Chicago as a dancer and model. At Peoria's Cabaret Music Theatre, she quickly became an audience favorite, performing in numerous musical productions. Di-Anne has national television and radio credits and a part in the movie *Jo Jo Dancer, Your Life is Calling*, with Richard Pryor.

Comments: With easy access from all directions, Zellmer's is conveniently close to other area attractions: Wildlife Prairie Park, Peoria's Par-A-Dice Riverboat Casino, Casino Rick Island, paddle-wheeler cruises, antique and specialty shopping, plus fine hotels and dining.

CHAPTER 7

Dinner Theatre Directory

The following is a list of dinner theatres across the country, including, for each theatre, the address, telephone number, and union and association affiliations. An asterisk denotes that the dinner theatre is under the Actors' Equity/ADTI contract for the employment of union actors. A theatre's membership in the ADTI (American Dinner Theatre Institute) and the NDTA (National Dinner Theatre Association) membership is indicated.

ALASKA

Alaska Cabin Night
McKinley Chalet Resort
Denali National Park, AK 99755
(907) 683-2215
(NDTA)

ARIZONA

Gaslight Theatre
7010 E. Broadway
Tucson, AZ 85710
(602) 296-0456

ARKANSAS

Murry's Dinner Playhouse
6323 Asher Ave.
Little Rock, AR 72204
(501) 562-3131
(NDTA)

CALIFORNIA

Curtain Call Dinner Theatre
690 El Camino Real
Tustin, CA 92680
(714) 838-1540

Garbeau's Dinner Theatre
12401 Folsom Blvd.
Rancho Cordova, CA 95742-6413
(916) 985-6361
(NDTA)

Griswold's Candlelight Pavilion
555 W. Foothill Blvd.
Claremont, CA 91711
(714) 626-2411
(NDTA)

Lawrence Welk Resort Theatre*
8860 Lawrence Welk Dr.
Escondido, CA 92026
(619) 749-3000

Roger Rocka's Music Hall
1226 N. Wishon Ave.
Fresno, CA 93728
(209) 266-9493

Showboat Dinner Theatre
19817 Ventura Blvd.
Woodland Hills, CA 91364
(818) 884-7461

COLORADO

Ascot Dinner Theatre
9136 West Bowles Ave.
Littleton, CO 80123
(303) 972-0312
(ADTI, associate member; NDTA)

Boulder's Dinner Theatre
5501 Arapahoe
Boulder, CO 80302
(303) 449-6000

Country Dinner Playhouse*
P.O. Box 3167
Englewood, CO 80155
(303) 799-0112
(NDTA)

Heritage Square Music Hall
No. 5 Heritage Square
Golden, CO 80401
(303) 279-7800

CONNECTICUT

Connecticut's Broadway Theatre*
(formerly Darien Dinner Theatre)
65 Tokeneke Rd.
Darien, CT 06820
(203) 655-7667
(ADTI)

FLORIDA

Alhambra Dinner Theatre*
12000 Beach Blvd.
Jacksonville, FL 32216
(904) 641-1212
(ADTI)

Golden Apple Dinner Theatre*
25 N. Pineapple Ave.
Sarasota, FL 33577
(813) 366-2646
(ADTI)

Golden Apple Dinner Theatre*
447 U.S. 41 Bypass N.
Venice, FL 34292
(813) 366-2646
(ADTI)

Jupiter Theatre*
1001 E. Indiantown Rd.
Jupiter, FL 33477
(407) 747-5261
(NDTA)

Mark Two Dinner Theatre*
3376 Edgewater Dr.
Orlando, FL 32804
(407) 843-6275
(NDTA)

Naples Dinner Theatre
1025 Piper Blvd.
Naples, FL 33942
(813) 597-6031
(NDTA)

Royal Palm Dinner Theatre*
303 Golfview Dr.
Boca Raton, FL 33432
(305) 426-2211
(ADTI)

Showboat Dinner Theatre*
3405 Ulmerton Rd.
Clearwater, FL 34622
(813) 573-3777
(ADTI)

Tierra Verde Dinner Theatre
200 Madonna Blvd.
Tierra Verde, FL 33715
(813) 867-0257

ILLINOIS

Candlelight Dinner Playhouse*
5620 S. Harlem Ave.
Summit, IL 60501
(813) 597-6031
(ADTI)

Circa '21 Dinner Playhouse
1828 3rd Ave., Box 3784
Rock Island, IL 61204
(309) 786-2667
(NDTA)

Conklin Players Dinner Theatre
Box 301, Conklin Ct.
Goodfield, IL 61742
(309) 786-2667
(ADTI associate member)

Drury Lane Dinner Theatre*
2500 W. 95th St.
Evergreen Park, IL 60642
(708) 422-8000
(ADTI)

Drury Lane Oakbrook Terrace
    Theatre*
100 Drury Lane
Oakbrook Terrace, IL 60181
(708) 530-8300
(ADTI)

Marriott's Lincolnshire Theatre*
10 Marriott Dr.
Lincolnshire, IL 60069
(708) 634-0204
(ADTI)

Sunshine Dinner Playhouse
115 W. Kirby
Champaign, IL 61820
(217) 359-4503
(NDTA)

Zellmer's Main Street Dinner Theatre
45 N. Main St.
Farmington, IL 61531
(309) 245-2554
(NDTA)

INDIANA

Beef 'N Boards Dinner Theatre*
9301 N. Michigan Rd.
Indianapolis, IN 46268
(317) 872-9664
(NDTA)

Derby Dinner Playhouse
525 Marriott Dr.
Clarksville, IN 47130
(812) 288-2632
(NDTA)

Good Times Theatre
Rte. 1, Box 180B
Bryant, IN 47326
(800) 288-7630
(NDTA)

IOWA

Ingersoll Dinner Theatre
3711 Ingersoll Ave.
Des Moines, IA 50312
(515) 274-5582
(NDTA)

KANSAS

Crown Uptown Dinner Theatre
3207 E. Douglas
Wichita, KS 67218
(316) 681-1566
(NDTA)

New Theatre Restaurant*
9229 Foster
Overland Park, KS 66212-6177
(816) 561-7529

LOUISIANA

New Rose Dinner Playhouse
201 Robert St.
Gretna, LA 70056
(504) 376-5400

MARYLAND

Act Two Dinner Theatre
8014 Pulaski Hwy.
Baltimore, MD 21237
(301) 686-1126

Burn Brae Dinner Theatre
15029 Blackburn Rd.
Burtonsville, MD 20866
(301) 384-5800

Harborlights Dinner Theatre
511 S. Broadway
Baltimore, MD 21231
(301) 522-4126

Harlequin Dinner Theatre
1330 E. Gude Dr.
Rockville, MD 20850
(301) 340-6813

Oregon Ridge Dinner Theatre
13403 Beaver Dam Rd.
Cockeysville, MD 21030
(401) 771-8427

Toby's Dinner Theatre
Box 1003
Columbia, MD 21044
(301) 730-8311
(NDTA)

Towsontowne Dinner Theatre
7800 York Rd.
Towson, MD 21204
(401) 321-6595

MASSACHUSETTS

Medieval Manor Theatre Restaurant
246 East Berkeley St.
Boston, MA 02118
(617) 423-4900

Mystery Cafe Dinner Theatre
11 Green St.
Boston, MA 02130
(617) 524-2233

MICHIGAN

Cornwell's Dinner Theatre
P.O. Box 734
Marshall, MI 49068
(616) 781-7933
(NDTA)

Golden Lion Dinner Theatre
22380 Moross Rd.
Detroit, MI 48026
(313) 886-2420

MINNESOTA

Chanhassen Dinner Theatre*
501 W. 78th Ave.
Chanhassen, MN 55317
(612) 934-1525
(ADTI)

MISSOURI

American Heartland Theatre*
2450 Grand Ave.
Kansas City, MO 64108
(816) 842-9999

NEBRASKA

Firehouse Dinner Theatre
514 S. 11th St.
Omaha, NE 68102
(402) 346-6009

NEW JERSEY

Castle Dinner Theatre
P.O. Box 69
Hamburg, NJ 07419
(201) 827-0112

Neil's New Yorker Dinner Theatre
90 Route 46
Mountain Lakes, NJ 07046
(201) 627-1865

NEW YORK

Beck's Grove Dinner Theatre
P.O. Box 428
Middle Island, NY 11953
(516) 732-2240

Island Squire Dinner Theatre
P.O. Box 428
Middle Island, NY 11953
(516) 732-2240

Lake George Dinner Theatre*
P.O. Box 4623
Queensbury, NY 12804
(518) 761-1092

Westchester Broadway Theatre*
(formerly An Evening Dinner Theatre)
1 Broadway Plaza
Elmsford, NY 10523
(914) 592-2268
(ADTI)

NORTH CAROLINA

Barn Dinner Theatre
120 Stagecoach Trail
Greensboro, NC 27409
(919) 292-2211

Triangle Dinner Theatre
P.O. Box 12168
Research Triangle Park, NC 27709
(919) 549-8951

OHIO

Carousel Dinner Theatre*
1275 E. Waterloo Rd.
Akron, OH 44306
(216) 724-9855
(ADTI, NDTA)

La Comedia Dinner Theatre
P.O. Box 204
Springboro, OH 45066
(513) 746-3114
(NDTA)

OREGON

Sylvia's Class Act
5115 Northeast Sandy Blvd.
Portland, OR 97213
(503) 288-6828

PENNSYLVANIA

Conley's Dinner Theatre
Route 30
Irwin, PA 15642
(412) 863-0700

David Group
3083 Altonah Rd.
Bethlehem, PA 18017
(215) 868-0056

Dutch Apple Dinner Theatre
510 Centerville Rd.
Lancaster, PA 17601
(717) 898-1900
(NDTA)

Genetti Dinner Playhouse
Route 309
Hazleton, PA 18201
(717) 454-2494
(NDTA)

Huntingdon Valley Dinner Theatre
2633 Philont Ave.
Huntingdon Valley, PA 19006
(215) 947-6000

Riverfront Dinner Theatre
Delaware Ave. at Poplar St.
Philadelphia, PA 19123
(215) 925-7000

Rockwell Grand Candlelight Theatre
32 South Turbot Ave.
Milton, PA 17847
(717) 742-2511
(NDTA)

Shawnee Playhouse
P.O. Box 159
Shawnee-on-Delaware, PA 18356
(717) 421-5093

TENNESSEE

Chaffin's Barn
8204 Hwy. 100
Nashville, TN 37221
(615) 646-9977
(ADTI, associate member; NDTA)

VIRGINIA

Barksdale Dinner Theatre
P.O. Box 7
Hanover, VA 23069
(804) 537-5333

Omni Dinner Theatre
777 Waterside Dr.
Norfolk, VA 23510
(804) 627-7773

Swift Creek Mill Playhouse
P.O. Box 41
Colonial Heights, VA 23834
(804) 748-5203

West End Dinner Theatre
4615 Duke St.
Alexandria, VA 22304
(703) 370-2500
(ADTI, associate member; NDTA)

WISCONSIN

Classic Arts
110 S. Nicolet Rd.
Appleton, WI 54915
(414) 734-2787
(NDTA)

Fanny Hill Inn and Dinner Theatre
3919 Crescent Ave.
Eau Claire, WI 54703
(715) 836-8141

Fireside Dinner Playhouse
P.O. Box 7
Ft. Atkinson, WI 53538
(414) 563-9505
(NDTA)

Northern Lights Playhouse
P.O. Box 256
Hazelhurst, WI 54531
(715) 356-7173
(NDTA)

CHAPTER 8

Informational Sources

The following is a list of various organizations, associations, publications, and suppliers that are involved with the dinner theatre industry and that the reader may find useful as sources of information.

ORGANIZATIONS AND ASSOCIATIONS

Actors' Equity Association (AEA)
165 West 46th St.
New York, NY 10036
(212) 869-8530

Alliance of Resident Theatres/
New York
131 Varick St., Room 904
New York, NY 10013

American Bus Association
1015 15th St. N.W., Suite 250
Washington, D.C. 20005

American Dinner Theatre Institute
(ADTI)
P.O. Box 7057
Akron, OH 44306
(216) 724-8605

American Directors Institute (ADI)
248 West 74th St., Suite 10
New York, NY 10023

American Federation of Television
and Radio Artists (AFTRA)
260 Madison Ave.
New York, NY 10016

American Society of Composers,
Authors and Publishers (ASCAP)
1 Lincoln Plaza
New York, NY 10023

American Theatre Wing
250 West 57th St.
New York, NY 10107

Arts Management
408 West 57th St.
New York, NY 10019

Association of Theatrical Press
  Agents and Managers
165 West 46th St.
New York, NY 10036

BMI
320 West 57th St.
New York, NY 10019

Business Committee for the Arts
1775 Broadway, Suite 510
New York, NY 10019

Center for the Arts Information
1285 Ave. of the Americas, 3d Floor
New York, NY 10019

Costume Society of America
55 Edgewater Dr.
P.O. Box 73
Earleville, MD 21919

Dramatists Guild
234 West 44th St.
New York, NY 10036

Foundation for the Community of
  Artists
280 Broadway, Suite 412
New York, NY 10007

Foundation for the Extension and
  Development of the Professional
  Theatre (FEDAPT)
270 Lafayette St., Suite 810
New York, NY 10012

International Alliance of Theatrical
  Stage Employees (IATSE)
1515 Broadway, Suite 601
New York, NY 10036

League of Chicago Theatres and
  Chicago Theatre Foundation
  (LCT and CTF)
22 West Monroe St., Suite 801
Chicago, IL 60603

National Alliance of Musical Theatre
  Producers
330 W. 45th St., Lobby B
New York, NY 10036
(212) 265-5376

National Assembly of Local Arts
  Agencies
1420 K Street, Suite 204
Washington, D.C. 20005

National Dinner Theatre Association
  (NDTA)
c/o Derby Dinner Playhouse
525 Marriott Dr.
Clarksville, IN 47130
(812) 288-2632

National Endowment for the Arts and
  Humanities
1100 Pennsylvania Ave. N.W.
Washington, D.C. 20506

National Federation of Independent
  Business
150 W. 20th Ave.
San Mateo, CA 94403

National Restaurant Association
  (NRA)
1200 Seventeenth St. N.W.
Washington, D.C. 20036-3097

National Tour Association, Inc.
546 E. Main St.
Lexington, KY 40508

Professional Arts Management Institute
408 West 57th St.
New York, NY 10019

Screen Actors Guild (SAG)
7065 Hollywood Blvd.
Hollywood, CA 90028

Society of Stage Directors and Choreographers (SSDC)
1501 Broadway, 31st Floor
New York, NY 10036
(212) 391-1070

Southeastern Theatre Conference (SETC)
University of North Carolina at Greensboro
506 Stirling St.
Greensboro, NC 27412

Theatre Library Association
111 Amsterdam Ave.
New York, NY 10023

United Scenic Artists
575 Eighth Ave.
New York, NY 10018

Volunteer Lawyers for the Arts (VLT)
1285 Ave. of the Americas, 3d Floor
New York, NY 10019

PUBLICATIONS

Back Stage
P.O. Box 41489
Nashville, TN 37204-1489
(800) 999-3322 (subscriptions)

Byways (National Motorcoach Network)
Patriot Square
10527C Braddock Rd.
Fairfax, VA 22032

Nation's Restaurant News
P.O. Box 31197
Tampa, FL 33633-0691

Restaurant Business
Circulation Dept.
633 Third Ave.
New York, NY 10017-6743

Restaurant Hospitality
1100 Superior Ave.
Cleveland, OH 44114-2543

Restaurant USA
1200 Seventeenth St., NW
Washington, D.C. 20036-3097

Restaurant/Hotel Design
633 Third Ave.
New York, NY 10017

Restaurants & Institutions
Cahner Plaza
1350 E. Touhy Ave.
P.O. Box 5080
Des Plaines, IL 60017-5080

Theatre Crafts
135 Fifth Ave.
New York, NY 10010

Travel Agent
825 Seventh Ave.
New York, NY 10019

Variety
Subscription Dept.
P.O. Box 710
Brewster, NY 10509-9864
(914) 878-7269 (subscriptions)

PROFESSIONAL REFERENCES

A large number of restaurant-related books of potential interest to the dinner theatre operator are available from:

Van Nostrand Reinhold
Mail Order Dept.
P.O. Box 668
Florence, KY 41022-9979
(800) 926-2665

SUPPLIERS AND MISCELLANEOUS

Agency for the Performing Arts, Inc.
  (APA)
888 Seventh Ave.
New York, NY 10106
(212) 582-1500

Akin, Gump, Hauer & Feld
Lawrence Levien, Attorney
1333 New Hampshire Ave. N.W.
Washington, D.C. 20036
(202) 887-4054

Dramatists Play Service, Inc.
440 Park Ave. South
New York, NY 10016
(212) 683-8960

Music Theatre International
545 Eighth Ave.
New York, NY 10018
(212) 868-66688

Norcostco
3203 North Hwy. 100
Minneapolis, MN 55422-9975

Rodgers and Hammerstein Musical
  Library
1633 Broadway, Suite 3801
New York, NY 10019
(212) 541-6600

Samuel French, Inc.
45 West 25th St.
New York, NY 10010
(212) 206-8990

Tams-Witmark Music Library, Inc.
560 Lexington Ave.
New York, NY 10022
(212) 688-2525

Triad
10100 Santa Monica Blvd.,
  Suite 1600
Los Angeles, CA 90067
(310) 556-2727

William Morris Agency/New York
1350 Ave. of the Americas
New York, NY 10019
(212) 586-5100

Index

About the Author

WILLIAM M. LYNK is a columnist on dinner theatre for *Back Stage* and former Executive Director of the American Dinner Theatre Institute and publicist for the nation's largest dinner theatre, Carousel Dinner Theatre in Akron, Ohio. He has also written, produced and directed television commercials, radio spots, and video productions and published and lectured widely on many aspects of the entertainment industry.